I Am Therefore I Am

Finding God in our Heart

LAWRENCE DOOCHIN

I Am Therefore I Am
Finding God In Our Heart

© 2008 Lawrence Doochin

All rights reserved. No portion of this book may be reproduced in whole or in part, by any means whatever, except for passages excerpted for purposes of review, without the prior written permission of the publisher. For information please contact:

In Harmony Publishing
lawrence@lawrencedoochin.com

Doochin, Lawrence.

   I am therefore I am : finding God in our heart / Lawrence Doochin. -- 1st ed. -- Franklin, Tenn. : In Harmony Pub., c2008.
     p. ; cm.

   ISBN: 978-0-9816990-5-9

   1. God--Love. 2. Love--Religious aspects. 3. Spiritual life. I. Title.

BT140 .D66 2008   2008926005
231.042--dc22   0804

2 4 6 8 9 7 5 3 1

First edition

I dedicate this book to my beautiful wife Janice and our children Sarah, Thomas, David, and Hannah. Janice, you have put up with a lot from me and you have loved me throughout. Thank you for your love and support and for telling me what I needed to hear, even when I didn't want to hear it. To my kids, you have been a blessing in our lives. Thank you for loving unconditionally and for helping me to remember who I really am. I also dedicate this book to God. Your Love has cleansed me and I have been reborn in it. Without that Love, I would not exist.

Acknowledgements

I want to thank all of the angels who have come in to my life and who have helped me to move along this path with grace and certainty. You have always come exactly at the moment I needed you. This is the second version of this book which contains the revelations, and I was assisted greatly by my publicist, Mari Selby, and my editor, Heather Froeschl. Thank you for your inspiration and wisdom.

Table of Contents

Foreword..1
CHAPTER 1 Appearance and Belief 8
CHAPTER 2 Perfection..........................16
CHAPTER 3 Faith...............................19
CHAPTER 4 The Will of God.....................22
CHAPTER 5 Expansiveness 26
CHAPTER 6 Recognition and Remembrance.........28
CHAPTER 7 Paradox 31
CHAPTER 8 Contrast............................35
CHAPTER 9 Know Thyself........................38
CHAPTER 10 A Puzzle............................41
CHAPTER 11 Power...............................44
CHAPTER 12 Experience 47
CHAPTER 13 Thought.............................50
CHAPTER 14 Meaning of Life.....................52
CHAPTER 15 What is Real........................55
CHAPTER 16 The Good Stuff Fear, Anger,
           Self Judgment, Guilt, and Shame.....58
CHAPTER 17 The One.............................66
CHAPTER 18 Understanding.......................71
CHAPTER 19 Our Purpose 74
CHAPTER 20 The Spiritual Journey 77
CHAPTER 21 A Poem 86
CHAPTER 22 Illusion and Truth..................87
CHAPTER 23 Of Yourself.........................91
CHAPTER 24 The Light 94
CHAPTER 25 Sin and Sacrifice 97
CHAPTER 26 The Mind...........................102
CHAPTER 27 The Witness........................108
CHAPTER 28 Duality 110
CHAPTER 29 Creation...........................112
CHAPTER 30 Love 117
AUTHOR'S NOTE 126
FURTHER STEPS ALONG THE JOURNEY 128

Foreword

May these pages lead you to non understanding, for God is infinite. How can we understand something which is infinite?

For the first thirty years of my life, I had no observable relationship with, and felt no connection to, God. My earliest memory on this journey is one of putting my oldest daughter, who was around two years old at that time, down for a nap, and I felt such immense Love for her. And I said thank you God, from my heart, with true gratitude, for the first time in my life. This was when I knew, for the first time, that Love was the most powerful force in the universe.

The revelations contained in this book were only a beginning for me; a further unfolding on my path of Love. It was not as if I received these revelations on a mountaintop and I shouted them to the masses. I knew that they were given to me to help me, and whether they had application elsewhere, I could not say at the time. As I began to live these revelations and they were integrated in my own experience, their logic is what first appealed to me, allowing "acceptance" by my mind.

Somehow, through God's Grace, this acceptance created the space for my mind to take periodic vacations or short periods when I simply was; I was present in the holy moment. At first, this scared me, as I felt that if these periods continued to increase, I would lose my mind, lose my ability to function. But, again, through the Grace of God, I was able to realize that living in the present is our natural state, one which brings us the greatest joy and peace. I realized that my mind, my strong intellect, was still there for me to use when I chose to do so. As I let Life be where it is, for me and everyone else, I began to walk more frequently on the path of Love, where my heart, not my mind, gave me sight; a sight of unending beauty, gentleness, and Love. When you begin to experience Oneness with that Love, you look back with a sense of wonder, awe, and extreme gratitude, at how you arrived at this point in life. Unbeknownst to any of us at the time, God awakens our heart with a seed of Love. Eventually, the seed, having been nourished with Light and with the sustenance of whole vision, will unfold into its fullness, blossoming into a flower which offers magnificent beauty and peace for those who encounter it. Some people are awakened early in life, while others, needing to go through certain experiences which will prepare the heart for implanting, wait a little longer. I was one who waited a little longer.

There is no right or wrong way to read this book, although I suggest that you do not skip ahead the first time you read it. Some may read the book only once, while others may return to the pages, time and time again. If you are encountering a particularly difficult situation, you may want to use a bookmark or some other means of turning randomly to a page, allowing God to present to you the chapter and the particular statement that can be of help. If you use this method, you will know which statement is the one for you at that time, especially if it brings up a reaction in you.

The true nature of God and of ultimate reality is beyond description. However, communication, or statements such as these, can be stepping stones that place us on the path toward full remembrance of our true nature. Our beliefs are very entrenched, especially the core belief, the belief in separation. When we examine our beliefs by looking in to how they came about, we become less rigid and we open ourselves up to experience God, for Creation is fluid. There is some redundancy in the statements, and where repetition is present, it enables the Light of Truth to shine on those false beliefs from several different angles and perspectives, eventually dissolving those beliefs in the Light. You may notice some apparent contradictions in the statements. Existence is a paradox. We cannot escape that, nor would we want to, because staying present in the paradox carries us toward remembrance. If you get stuck on two seemingly opposite statements, allow yourself the freedom of releasing judgment and put the issue to the back burner until you finish the book. You can always come back to it. After you have read each statement, give it time to sink in. You may want to sit with it for a while, or you may be ready for the next statement. Realize that the space between the words and between the statements and the stillness that is present in that space is as important as the words themselves, for this action/non action cycle is the crux of our existence.

Finally, feel free to substitute God with whatever word you feel most comfortable with. I refer to God as both Him and Her, because the Divine truly encompasses both the male and female energies.

If you take anything in the book as absolute, and say to yourself that you must always see it that way, it leads to a belief, and the purpose here is to remove, not to add something else which is false. There can be no absolutes, because the manifestation of God in form is constantly changing, constantly being recreated. Our lives and this spiritual journey appear as a continuum, one in which we can never be at one set point. Allow the River of Life to move you up and down the continuum. The scenery changes each moment, but the River stays the same. This is the stillness, the Absolute that underlies all that is. As you move along the River, it helps tremendously when you can laugh at the scenery as well as at yourself.

You will sense a natural progression within the pages, mirroring my journey with these revelations as well as one that you may be on, and you may strongly identify with certain statements. This is simply an area of the continuum that you have already visited or are ready to visit, and the revelation becomes "true" for you within the context of where you are. Sometimes it will seem that you are moving up and down the continuum in a straight line, and other times it will appear more like a spiral or a circle.

Allow the words to deepen your recognition of your relationship with God, because these revelations do not belong solely to me. They were given to me as part of my journey of remembrance, my path of God pulling me closer to Him, but each of us is a manifestation of the One, and these revelations are our birthright. When you are hungry, God feeds that hunger. These revelations could have found their way to you through an infinite number of ways, including them being revealed in your own consciousness, and you are being fed every moment of every day, in many ways you may not yet recognize.

I spoke earlier about putting my daughter to sleep and knowing that Love was the most powerful force in the Universe. This was my first glimpse of the mountaintop, but usually that first view takes place at the base of the mountain. I had no way of knowing at that time that I had a long climb ahead of me. If we know exactly what the journey entails, the joys **and** the sorrows, the suffering, and the fear, then we might not undertake the journey. For a long time I wanted to know what lay ahead for me, but I finally realized that it is much more fun to be surprised. When you constantly look to the future, you do it out of fear and a need to control, and you miss the beauty and peace of the present moment, even if in that present moment you experience suffering. My journey took many twists and turns, including many descents into emotional hell. I began intense emotional therapy regarding an issue with my mother at the same time that God had awakened me with the seed of Love. I thought that I was on two separate paths, an emotional path and a spiritual path, and that these paths would come together at some point in my life. I now realize that it was always one path. The emotions are the gateway to the spirit. God is Love, and Creation is an expression of that Love. When we love, we are like God. We are "GIA" - God in action. You experience the joy and peace of God to the extent that you have worked through those emotional blockages related to childhood issues. As you release false beliefs about yourself, you reveal the God within.

I have no advanced degrees in theology. My only qualifications were that I had a deep longing for Truth and for God, and I suspect that since you have picked up this book, that is the case for you. Life has been my greatest teacher, and I am especially grateful to my family, my wife and four children, who have acted as mirrors into my Self.

A number of prosperity books have been written in the last few years, and it is important to know that thought is creative and this is how the Universe works. These books are important steps on the path to God, but this is an evolutionary process. We are meant to go further, and we must go further. This world is a dream, and while it is fine to create what you want, this is *not* what you truly want. You can enjoy the material possessions and the dream job, but these will give you an illusory happiness, for true happiness comes from inside of you and is based on your Oneness with God. Only His Love will fulfill you, and every experience in this dream is meant to bring you to that recognition along with a remembrance of that Love.

Finally, it is my hope that these statements will provide a place of comfort for you on your spiritual journey, because the journey can be difficult at times. Since I have lived these revelations as part of my experience, I have interwoven my journey into the statements where applicable. Sometimes it is enough just knowing that someone else has walked the same path, has gone through similar trials, and has lost faith while in the valley. My gift to you is this book, and because every relationship is reciprocal, I thank you for the blessing of Love that you have bestowed upon me by picking up the book, for as you read the pages, we both increase our remembrance. In the end, this book and the purpose for its existence, the reason that I was given these revelations along with caretaker responsibility, and the reason that they have found their way to you, is about Love. As you sit in the stillness with the words, you will be able to hear God calling you, God embracing you, you whom are His Beloved. And you will return the call, for this is what your heart has always longed for.

☥

CHAPTER 1

Appearance and Belief

Because of the issue with my mother and other childhood traumas, I saw the world through the eyes of a scared boy who had been hurt, although I certainly did not recognize this for a long time. The teen years are ones where it is important to build self confidence, but this did not happen for me since I was emotionally frozen in an earlier time. Just as we progress physically, we must progress emotionally. During those teen years and throughout my twenties, I played the "game." I exhibited a strong self confidence, a strong ego, but this was only an outer covering over the frightened little boy who was crying for love and comfort. Sadly, my experience is similar to a large number of people living today. The beliefs that I carried about myself were that I was not worthy, not lovable, not a good person. I also felt very guilty and shameful. Because I could not feel any relationship with God, I did not know that I could turn to Him for comfort and for a proper modeling of what unconditional Love meant. So I continued on through the pain of daily life, always looking at the world and what happened to me through the filter of what had taken place in my childhood. Bluntly, I saw the world as unforgiving, and I saw a strong split between good and evil, of which I was a part of the latter and for which I needed punishment. This never came in to my awareness, because

APPEARANCE AND BELIEF

it would have destroyed the whole foundation on which my false self was built, and I was not ready for that. But these underlying beliefs were still directing my thoughts, my actions, and how I saw the world. When the beliefs are hidden, they have a stronger influence than if they are at the surface. One is like a robot with a certain software program running which one is unaware of and can do nothing about. A virus. Finally, I was given the gift of my children, because they acted like mirrors in to my self. As I raged against them and my wife, I saw that I was really raging about how I felt about myself. As they progressed through certain stages in childhood, this helped me to remember my childhood. I began to see behind the lens of my beliefs and I began to bring those beliefs to the surface. As I gradually cleared those false beliefs, the true appearance of the world started to reveal itself.

☥

What is the difference between the following statements? The world is as I see it. I see the world as it is.

Perception is a fine line, a line that is walked in each moment as we are constantly bombarded with stimuli from the world. Are we seeing what is true and real, or are we simply perceiving through our senses what we think is going on? If you assume that the world *is* as you see it, then your filters---your experiences, your beliefs, your perceptions, your senses that are unique to your body---are distorting what you see. It is as if you are looking at the world with rose colored glasses. For instance, if your experience has been one where

9

you had a close relative who was murdered, then it is likely that you will favor capital punishment more than a person who has not had a similar experience. But what if the same murder of a close relative was the vehicle for you to open your heart in forgiveness of the murderer? What if, through forgiveness, you became friends with the murderer and you were grateful for the changes that had occurred in your heart and in your life? You probably would not be a proponent of capital punishment. So, what is the truth about this murder? Is it a horrific crime, an unfortunate act that leads to healing, or both? Or do none of them apply? It is evident that an act has occurred, but it is the filters of each person which take that simple act further. The filters, the beliefs, the experiences assign a meaning that is not there. If you step back from those filters, you see only an act or event. I see the world as it is. I see the act as it is, not the act is as I see it.

The above example included capital punishment, certainly an emotional issue in this society. Did you have a reaction when you read the above? If not this issue, what issue triggers a reaction within you? Regardless of whether you openly express a reaction, and regardless of whether you can recognize reactions that occur within you, everyone walking this Earth is in a physical body which has primal urges and everyone has a mind which is conditioned by its past. Are you your beliefs, or are you something more? It has been demonstrated with the above example that there can be strongly divergent perceptions (beliefs) about the same event. Are we all looking at the same tree but from different perspectives? Maybe some of us are at root level, while others are mid trunk, and others are in the treetops (lucky them).

Think about beliefs that you strongly hold. Where did this belief system originate? It originated in the past, from experiences you have had, consciously or unconsciously. Your belief system also originates from expectations you have about the future. You believe that life will be a certain way in the future. You believe that you will have a family, a certain career, or that your body will look a certain way. Each of us has a belief system that is constructed from our *own* experiences and our *own* expectations about the future. If each of us has a different perspective, what is reality? Are we seeing the whole tree, or are we just seeing the roots? And do we join groups that affirm our belief system because that makes us feel better that our beliefs are "right?" Maybe those who agree with our beliefs are simply those people who are also seeing only the roots and not the whole tree. And when those who live in the treetops call out and say what they see, those down at the roots become fearful, because they say that this couldn't be possible. They don't see the same view, but all they need to do is back up to a different perspective so they can see the whole tree. The greater your fear, the more you are attached to your belief system. As fear increases, you become hardened in your beliefs, and you look for others who hold the same belief to validate what is only a perception, what is only one perspective. When you are part of a group, it seems as if your fear is alleviated and as if you have a sense of security, but this is impossible.

Our beliefs produce a perspective where we see good and bad, where we see differences. The whole world, every experience, every choice, even every thought revolves around the contrast created through good and bad. But isn't good and bad subject to each of our own interpretations? Is alcoholism bad if it tears apart a family, or could it be good if, through recovery, it is the impetus for healing, just like the murder example? Could the alcoholism be partially bad and partially good? Do you see how confusing this can become? What if your boss at work yells at you for poor performance? If you feel good about yourself and you know that you are an excellent worker, then you will probably let the comment go without dwelling on it. But if you are unsure of yourself, then the comment will add to the uncertainty. The same comment takes on a different meaning according to your beliefs. In fact, it can take on an infinite number of meanings. Obviously, when we talk about beliefs, there are no absolutes. We are on shifting ground. We are on a foundation of sand.

To summarize, appearances contain contrast. Their foundation is "good" and "bad." But this leads to a belief about appearances which is not real. If appearances are not real, what *is* Real? What is changeless that underlies all appearances? Surely, something must be changeless, or the universe would be utter chaos. At this point you might say that this world does exhibit chaos, but it is the *appearance* of the world which exhibits chaos, as seen through the eyes of the beholder. The world seems to change every instant, yet it is the eyes of the beholder, individually and collectively as the human race, which change and which are the impetus for the apparent changes in the appearance of the world. To put it another way, as our beliefs change, the world seems to change.

When you cling to your beliefs out of fear, you cling to a rock in the River of Life, and the current repeatedly smashes you in to the rock. If you release your beliefs, or you at least witness them for what they are, then the current carries you along effortlessly. Life becomes much easier, much simpler. You know that you are moving toward this when you are able to laugh at your beliefs and at the intensity with which you held those beliefs.

Awareness of your beliefs is the key. Many of your beliefs, especially those about yourself, are hidden. If you do not see and clear negative or limiting beliefs about yourself, they will offset any positive beliefs that you hold. The degree to which and the duration that it takes to manifest a positive belief about yourself directly corresponds to the depth of your limiting beliefs and how consciously aware you are of those beliefs. Some of the deepest negative beliefs you have about yourself need to be brought into the light of your awareness numerous times before they are cleared. You encounter the same belief along a different part of the spiral, seeing its falsity from a different angle and with new vision.

The strongest negative belief held by individuals is self judgment. This is an individual's belief that he is not worthy, that he is not "good enough" as he is, and most people are not aware that they hold this belief. The world appears as it does from a collective self judgment. It is a projection or reflection of how each of us individually self judges. All judgment is self judgment, even if it appears to be directed to someone or something "outside" of you. The world is as you see it. You do not see the world and make judgment on it. You judge, and the world appears to take that shape and form to you.

Can this apply to our emotions as well? That is, are the feelings we have affected by our belief in them? Yes. The substance or energy behind all emotions is the same. When an energy rises within us, i.e. anger, we immediately identify it as anger. Our belief that it is anger *makes* it anger. The energy is neutral, but our belief gives support to the appearance of a certain outcome or result, which is then used as confirmation for the belief, creating a dog chasing his tail scenario. If you see it as only a neutral energy, you will short-circuit this cycle, allowing you to be the master of your emotions. Anger was a difficult emotion on my journey. I was a rager, acting just like a child throwing a temper tantrum. Following the rage came the guilt and self judgment that occurred when I had expressed the anger in a hurtful manner, especially at my wife and children. As long as I was self judging over the anger, I wasn't allowing it to be what it was. I was stuck in the cycle as self judgment created more anger. The anger only dissipated as I began to clear the belief behind it. What makes you angry, and what is the belief behind that anger?

So, what happens if we take away our beliefs and we see past appearances? Appearances consist of differences. If there are no differences, then there is only a single unified entity. God is One. This universal essence, this source of creative energy, cannot be divided. It can only *appear* to be divided, as evidenced by everything around you. But remember, appearances are not reality. Reality or Truth is not what you want it to be. It is

APPEARANCE AND BELIEF

not your beliefs, your perceptions, or judgments, because as shown, these are not universally held. Truth is indivisible and self evident.

When you know that God is One and that there is only this single unified entity, that God is all that exists, then you settle into a great peace. Because behind all appearances, behind the appearance that is you, only God exists. You are a part of this Oneness. This is not a great leap of faith. This is what you already are, what you know yourself to be when you begin to look at your beliefs and behind appearances. So, if each of us is a manifestation of God, why do we *appear* to be separate? For God to know Himself. The One, who is infinite and all that exists, can only know Himself by appearing to be finite, separate parts. God, who is Love, knows Himself, Loves Herself, through the appearance, the contrast. His expressing through, and as, "each" of us and through all Creation is the appearance. Our journey is like a puzzle, where we are the pieces appearing to be put back into place to restore completeness. Our remembrance that we are the Oneness helps us to look behind appearances, to look beyond our beliefs and see the truth, to see the world as it truly is and not to see it through the appearance that was created from our beliefs.

☥

CHAPTER 2

Perfection

I had to realize my imperfections before I could realize my perfection. As I went through therapy, I first uncovered my beliefs about myself, which then showed me what I considered to be my imperfections. As I tried to work on those imperfections, I was frustrated, because I was striving for something, perfection, which I could never reach. I could always be more loving to my wife and kids, but could I ever be a perfect husband and father? Not reaching that perfection led to self judgment, which was another imperfection that I judged. I was finally released from this never ending cycle when I changed my view of what perfection meant. Perfection is not a destination. One would never say that a certain piece of artwork is perfect, nor would one say that it is imperfect; it just is.

☥

The world sees perfection as an unreachable goal for a human being, because someone can always do or be better. You can always be more kind, more intelligent, or better looking. The world ascribes perfection to God and rightly so. But when we use the term "better," we fall back into the trap of assigning good and bad. Being intelligent is seen as good, while being dumb is seen as bad. When we get past the appearance to the energy that is God, perfection is what remains, and since we are manifestations of God in form, we are also that perfection. Know that your life, whatever the appearance, whether you are rich or poor, whether you are healthy or sick, is the highest expression of perfection possible. Only one expression of consciousness exists.

Everything is as it should be. It cannot be otherwise or it would not be perfect. Perfection is as it is.

As manifestations of God, we are the facets in the perfect diamond which is God, brilliantly reflecting off each other to show the magnificence of the diamond. An individual facet may *appear* to have a little covering of grime that needs to be cleaned, but the underlying brilliance is always there.

Should we help to improve the world? Should we speak out against injustice, selfishness, and greed? Should we cleanse our bodies and minds of toxicity and unhealthy emotional patterns? Should we cry out because most people turn their face from God, from their own true nature? Yes, while at the same time we recognize that all is perfect as it is.

God rests in His perfection, undisturbed in complete peace and tranquility. He has no need of anything, because His perfection encompasses everything and is complete by definition. This pattern of perfection is carried throughout all Creation. It is carried within you. If you continue to seek perfection outside of yourself, if you continue to seek something "better," you will live in sorrow and suffering, and you will have great frustration, because you will never find what you seek.

What does this perfection mean for everyone? Its significance is that each of us can finally accept ourselves as we are. And we can accept others exactly as they are. Did your belief system just creep back in? (Who was the person that just arose in your mind?) Perfection doesn't need to be changed. When you try to change someone, you are trying to change God. How successful do you think that will be?

Accepting the perfection also means the recognition that everything that arises within you is holy. Yes, that includes guilt, anger, fear, shame, and hatred.

If you are reading these words, are you meant to proceed on the journey, taking each step on the path or each bend in the river that Life brings to you so that you can continue increasing your awareness of your Oneness? Yes. Are you already complete and perfect in your awareness, knowing that no steps need to be taken and no journey needs to be traveled? Yes. Is this a difficult concept for you to accept? Therein lies the paradox.

CHAPTER 3

Faith

All spiritual journeys, including mine, are journeys of faith. It is the mortar which cements the building bricks of your life, allowing your house, your Consciousness to fully be built. The one constant on my journey, especially when I have suffered greatly, has been my faith, my trust in God's total benevolence and Love and in a greater purpose for my life. For there have been many times when I have struggled mightily against where the River was taking me, that I have felt as if everything, except faith, had been taken away from me. To put it another way, when everything false falls away, faith is all that remains. When out of fear I tried to cling to the rock in the River of Life, my faith was what finally allowed me to let go and move farther down the river, at least until the next set of rapids.

☥

Faith requires no understanding, for it is an intricate and inseparable part of your being. It is not something you acquire. It is something that you *remember* and is revealed to you on your journey back to God.

Complete faith knows that God's Will is always being done, no matter the circumstance, and that God's Will for you is a perfect expression of Love, revealing your true Self. What does this mean? It means that *every* circumstance, every experience you have has the purpose of showing you the immensity of God's Love for you. What if you get cancer or if a loved one dies at a young age? Will your faith still be there? Faith is the by-product of knowing that God's Will is expressing perfectly for you and everyone, always. It is the by-product of knowing that you are an inseparable part of the Oneness.

Faith is remembered and revealed through contrast, through those times when it appears that our faith is low and is strongly being tested. Even when the fog is thick around us, causing grave doubts, we can trust that the Sun of Light is always present and will burn the fog away, revealing a glistening splendor. As we float on the River of Life, our faith is solidified every time we let the current carry us effortlessly, as opposed to those times when we resist and cling to a rock or the shore. We will hit rocks in the River, but it is these questioning times, these doubting times, these times of non faith which open the gates of remembrance to an even deeper faith. When we bounce off the rock and we have faith in the River, when we have faith in God, we see that we will not drown, and we see that we will be completely taken care of. Just like a tree which is dormant during the winter and is preparing to flower, in our bleakest times, our times of winter, each of us prepares to flower. This is the time when significant inner discovery can be accomplished. While we are in the valley, it is our continuing faith in God and his Love that sees us through and allows his Will to be done.

In the early stages of your journey it appears as if your faith in God is built through inner experiences or "outside" events which happen to you. As you progress to a deeper remembrance of God, you realize that it is your faith which is creating these experiences or events, not the other way around. Also, as more of your true faith is uncovered, faith in what the world has to offer falls away. No longer do you look to material possessions or money as your God. Money holds a large preoccupation in this society, but money is only paper. Green paper. It is not the root of all evil, nor is it something to be worshipped. It is a medium of exchange, an energy of Love. You cannot eat it, wear it, or live under it. Yes, at present you can buy all of these things with money, but being able to do so operates under the premise that everyone has faith in money, in the system. And that is faith in a false God.

You finally reach a point on your faith journey where you see that there is no middle ground. Either you have complete faith that some entity created you---God, a Creator, a Great Spirit, a universal essence---that will completely Love and take care of you, or you have no faith whatsoever that this entity exists. There cannot be partial faith. If this entity exists, there can be no purpose for your existence other than to be loved completely.

☥

CHAPTER 4

The Will of God

One of the questions I have pondered the most is, what is God's Will for me. What does God want from me and how can I serve Him? Is God in control as it relates to the "bad" things that have happened to me? I struggled for a long time with this question as I tried to understand why my mother traumatized me. Was God working through my mother, or was this an act outside of His control? As I came to know that God works through each of us, I couldn't understand why this was done to me. Why did I have to suffer this pain? As I began to heal the emotional wounds and move deeper in to my spiritual journey, I still became frustrated when I couldn't ascertain His Will for me. While it appears there is a grand plan for my life, it also seems as if Truth and God exist outside of this plan, thus the plan does not matter. It has been difficult reconciling the two, not knowing what path and actions I should take and whether certain actions mean more than others. This paradox of our existence is discussed at greater length in chapter seven.

God is One, with nothing in opposition, and the Will of God is also One, all that exists.

The question arises, surely God does not will murder, rape, or child abuse. How can the will of a compassionate and loving God be compatible with evil? The answer that we hear most often is that we have free will, free choice without interference from God. But let's look deeper into this. Since God is One and we are a part of that Oneness, we are manifestations of God in form, thus God is making these choices through us. Do you have free choice, or do you have the appearance of free choice? If you truly had free choice, then you could be in opposition to the Will of God. But then God would not be One. You have only the appearance of free choice. Regardless of the appearance, everything that happens is God experiencing Itself through, and as, each of us. No experiences are better than others. It is your belief system which assigns better and worse. It is your belief system which this moment is fighting the Truth that nothing can be in opposition to the Will of God. It is your belief system which says separation must exist. As we progress in our remembrance of our Oneness, our actions and our experiences increasingly reflect the true essence of whom and what we are, which is Love. The mind which partakes in a murder may not remember its Oneness, but the experience is as holy for God as any other experience. Regardless of what form the experience takes, behind each form is God, is Love. So we reside in a paradox. Through choices we make in every moment, there is the appearance that we can be either in alignment or in opposition to God's Will, but at the same time every choice *is* God's Will, because this is all that exists.

When we can see God's Will for ourselves, we must release control and let God do the unfolding. Control comes from fear, but it is considerably more fun to be surprised by what the next bend in the River of Life brings to you. On the other side are the times when we may know that we are on a journey but we feel hopelessly lost and unable to discern God's Will. Some of our greatest advances and growth will come during these times, for we must trust in the unknown. We must have faith in the nothingness out of which all possibilities spring.

What does it mean to be completely fulfilled in God through Her Will? It means simply that you want God's Will to be done for you. You may get the prizes of the world. You may become rich, you may be in a loving relationship, but these are irrelevant. Only through doing Her Will, through Love, can you know that all of the Kingdom's riches, all peace, Love, and joy, have always been there for you.

Which would you choose? You can be extremely happy and joyful for the rest of your life, yet you are homeless. Or you can be very rich and powerful, even very well known, yet your level of happiness is an unknown. Which would you choose? Regardless of which one is your choice, it is a perfect expression of God's Will, and with that comes a great peace, a peace borne from the knowing that God's Will has no opposite.

With the recognition that God's Will is all that exists comes obedience to that Will. Obedience means surrender and recognition, surrender to the knowing that God's Love is all there is and that only by recognizing God's Will for you in each moment can you find true peace. Obedience means nothing of your self, so that you will fully shine *as* the Light of God.

☥

CHAPTER 5

Expansiveness

When I was a child, I would sit in bed at night and contemplate how the universe could be infinite. How can something go on forever? I would envision how there might be a brick wall in space where the universe would end, but then I would ask what was behind the wall. I would have to stop thinking about the whole idea because it would literally blow my mind. This concept of expansiveness, the concept that God is everywhere, without end, is unable to be understood and processed by a mind which is functioning in a body. The mind sees separation, and its perception is that time and space are fixed, but quantum physics has shown that they are not fixed. However, one advantage and purpose for being in a body, in a "separate" self, is that it gives us the perception we are limited, and this is the opening which provides the contrast to the infinite expansiveness that we are.

☥

A wave crashes on a distant beach that no one has ever visited. The wind blows through a stand of trees where no human has been. An ant moves in the forest. Ice sits buried twenty feet deep in Antarctica. All are God, one body, one Consciousness expressing joyfully. All are perfect, all are One, all appearing in different forms. This expression is continuous, whether seen or heard by humans. Expansiveness is *being* the Oneness with this expression that is throughout Earth and an infinite universe.

When you have been on the journey for a while, you can become frustrated as old belief systems return. Old fears, old judgments return, not to punish, but because they are Love, showing you who you really are through contrast. You can only know your expansiveness through comparison. The old beliefs are contained within expansiveness. Without any trees, there would be no recognition of a forest. Expansiveness is acceptance. How do you accept something which you believe is blocking you from the expansiveness? Understand that it is the *belief* that is blocking you—accept and embrace that belief.

Expansiveness holds everything and nothing. Everything, because it is all possibilities. Nothingness is from which the realm of all possibilities generates.

CHAPTER 6

Recognition and Remembrance

My recognition that I am something other than this personality in this body came in a flash, a moment out of time. Sure, I had read many books that told me I was something other than this human self, but I only knew that intellectually. As I often did, I was sitting in my car allowing the sadness to pour from me, and suddenly I was aware of another "self" within me, a self that was definitely me but that was also separate from the me I had known all my life. I looked down at my hands with amazement, like I was seeing them for the first time. This was my first awakening experience, and my remembrance grew gradually from that point on. As I have remembered that I am Love, I have increasingly recognized everything as either Love or a call for Love. This makes life very simple and joyous.

☥

Wouldn't it be great if you didn't have to change anything about yourself? If all you had to do were remember and recognize who you really are (did your body just affirm and recognize this Truth?) Change is not possible, for you eternally exist in Oneness with God. The light in you can never be extinguished, regardless of what false beliefs arise from your mind. On this earth you are a turtle pretending to be a fox, but you only need to remember that you are the turtle.

As part of the Oneness, everything you could ever possibly want—love, joy, peace—is available right here, right now in this moment. It is simply your recognition of this. Recognition of your true nature allows Creation to unfold with you as an intricate piece of the puzzle. Recognition allows Consciousness to awaken to Itself. It awakens the God within.

The world, especially western society, is enamored with learning, but we are not here to learn. A God that is Love cannot be known through the mind but rather through the heart. When we return to that remembrance, everything that is false falls away. Sometimes we actually have to forget what we have learned to create a space for remembrance to occur, and part of that is creating periods where we are still, either through meditation, quiet walks, or simply shutting off the television. If we cultivate a practice of remembrance in every moment, then every act, every thought, every breath becomes a meditation.

The journey that each of us is on is individualistic. You are your own path. You can borrow from spiritual traditions/histories or even from religion, and you can use what others have done before you to confirm, but you must be your own path. That is where your answers lie. It is a path of remembering created by you and God alone.

Can you do anything to increase your remembrance? There is nothing you can do to increase your remembrance except to let God lead you in each moment, and in whatever you are doing, there will be joy, for you are doing God's Will. If your actions spring from a belief that you should be doing something, either because others have done it or because you have done it in the past, there will not be joy present. However, you can recognize that your remembrance is spurred by periods of stillness, for these periods provide the contrast to the busyness of this society of which we are all a part. As your remembrance increases, you more frequently feel the presence of God, in, around, and as part of your Being, because this is your true nature. You do not have to isolate yourself, go to a retreat, or see a spiritual or religious mentor to feel His Presence. She is closer than your breath, and you can live this Presence in the ordinary workings of the day, the simplest of activities.

☥

CHAPTER 7

Paradox

One of the concepts that I have struggled with the most on my journey has been paradox. How could I be a perfect expression of God yet get angry or be unkind? How could I feel the Oneness with everything yet also see the differences?

☥

Are we human, or are we spirit? Are we One with God, or are we the Son? Opposite sides of the circle are still within the same circle.

How can two apparent opposites be true? The key word here is apparent. The paradox is always resolved in the One. One of the apparent opposites is contained within the other. The paradox of life is that only wholeness, perfection, and complete abundance exist within the One. Yet, we exist in bodies, in a world of duality where suffering exists. How can both be true? It is not how both can be true, but rather that the Truth contains both, because Truth contains all possibilities.

The energy, the blending of light and dark, is that which sustains life, which is the very source of life. God is One, with no distinctions, no differences. Yet, only through the paradox, through the appearance of differences, can God know Itself. Consciousness, our very being, relies on this contrast. One of the most apparent paradoxes is the appearance of a localized mind or ego that is present and functioning in a physical body and which is a consciousness that appears to be separate from a "God self" which knows no separation and no limits to its existence. Yet, only Oneness exists, and there cannot be two minds, two realities which function independently. There can be no split. But without the appearance of a difference, recognition would be impossible.

Do we use this localized mind, either through affirmations or positive statements, to redirect us back to our Oneness? God is beyond thought. God resides in the flowering of the heart, and if we stay in thought, we can never *be* that flowering. Yet, we exist as God taking form, and our mind is part of that form, a tool, similar to one used for building a house, to be used when appropriate. When the house is finished, all tools are put down, and we move in. But we pick up the tools occasionally as we continue to beautify where we live. As long as we live in a body, the mind will be necessary for organizing and functioning. This is not the same as understanding. Staying in the paradox opens us to the impossibility of understanding anything. For non-understanding is our true nature. To understand requires two of something. It requires that there be differences. It requires something being finite, and it is based on perception. Understanding is meaningless when God is One, nothing outside of Itself, infinite in nature.

When you remain in the paradox, you remain in balance. There is no black and white, because on the continuum which is Life, everything blends to grey. Balance allows for all possibilities, and it reflects the interplay of Oneness with the appearance of differences. Each person, as an expression of God, finds their own balance, and collectively, each group and each nation finds their own balance. You can never say something is absolutely right, because there are no absolutes, and there is only "right" for each individual. Only perfection exists, but finding your own balance means that you operate within the appearance of differences. You eat foods and exercise to help your body feel healthier. You seek counseling or therapy to express your feelings openly and to heal emotional wounds. You express love or perform service to make the world a better place. The degree to which you do or not do these actions is your own balance. By choosing to do certain actions, you are also choosing not to do other actions, and therein lies the balance which contains all possibilities. You are never stationary, always moving toward an action or non-action scenario through each choice you make. But whichever way you choose, that way could not be defined nor recognized without the other way being present. The appearance of healthy eating is only recognized when seen next to the appearance of unhealthy eating. The need for both to be present so that each can be recognized is the paradox.

The ultimate paradox is that we exist both as the One and the Son. Each of us is part of the Sonship, and without the Son, the One could not know Himself, could not Love Herself.

CHAPTER 8

Contrast

Contrast has been one of the most helpful tools along my path. For when I have been in the valley, when I have been in the fear, when I have been in that space that seems the opposite of Love, it is the contrast to the mountaintop of Love which illuminates and defines Love. Similarly, when I have exhibited regretful behavior toward my wife and kids, it is the contrast to that behavior which is a great teacher and shows me the behavior that I would prefer to exhibit the next time. These are two sides of the same coin. Everything around us is a world of richness, of contrast, and contrast shows us that there are no absolutes. Where I live, a seventy degree day in the middle of winter feels very warm, yet that same day in the middle of summer feels very cool. Contrast has revealed the very nature of God for me.

☥

God is stillness, but without the action, without the act of Creation, there could be no definition. It is the stillness/action cycle which defines God. This is the contrast inherent in duality. What the world sees as darkness is only contrast, not something to be judged. Without the darkness, light cannot be known. Only through contrast, can the light be defined. More contrast is not better nor worse---it just provides more definition. God is changeless, but through our belief in having an experience, it *seems* to happen. This gives the appearance of contrast to the changeless.

Our taking of form through a body and a mind provides a contrast to the infinite expansiveness that we are. It defines it, so that we can better know it. It is defined, so that God can better know Itself. A single star creates one point of recognition, of contrast, for an empty and dark universe. A multitude of stars enhances the experience a thousandfold.

The contrast show us who we are. When you think of yourself as the boat, you are rocked by every wave. You are not the boat. You are the ocean. Similarly, you are not the rollercoaster of Life. You are Life. If you think that you are the rollercoaster, you will be the ups and downs, the emotions and judgments that seem to banter you around like a rag doll. Be a witness to the rollercoaster, and you will be grateful for the gift it is giving to you. The bigger the rollercoaster, the more extreme the curves and the ups and downs, the greater the contrast to, and the greater your remembrance of, the infinite Allness that you are.

Without the contrast of opposites, there could be no recognition. Contained within each thought I have, each feeling I feel, each action I take, is its opposite, because the One is a continuum. When I am angry, peace is present also.

CONTRAST

When I experience fear, love is there. When I experience love, fear is there. Love cannot be recognized without the opposite of fear. Although they appear to be individual, each thought, action, feeling, or spoken word contains all possibilities as part of the continuum of Life.

☥

CHAPTER 9

Know Thyself

My tendency on this journey has been to look outside myself for the answers. This was especially true early on as I tried to find God. But as hard as I tried, I never found the answers in the world. When I looked outside myself, I would always seek but never find, for this world is not real, and thus it contains no answers. Looking outside myself was always painful, and this pain redirected me to look inside my Self and discover the treasure within. Increasingly, the false barriers of a bodily self gave way to the infinite expansiveness of my true Self, and knowing myself meant that there was only one of us to know. We are One in a sea of eternal spirit, completely safe, completely holy, and completely sinless.

☥

We are all on a journey of self discovery, regardless of our awareness of it. The descent into you is the descent into God. The Kingdom Of God begins and ends with you.

Know thyself *so* you can love one another. This is the joy inherent in the love that we are, in the reflection with other facets of the diamond that is God. Isolation reveals nothing, because without others, especially those close to you, there is no reflection. But when two mirrors are placed in front of each other, the reflection bounces back and forth, magnifying itself ad infinitum.

Our self is revealed in those reflections, those interactions with others. Everyone at one time or another has felt a strong need to tell or show someone something, especially if "it is for their own good." You may have told someone something that you think will improve their life, yet they disregard your advice and that upsets you. Your anger in this situation is a gift. The gift is a reflection that enables you to know yourself. Be still and let God show you where that need comes from inside of you. It will lead to a belief you have about yourself, a belief which you have attempted to hide through control of your life circumstances and control of those around you.

Close your eyes and imagine that you are awakening with complete amnesia. You have no memories, no past that gives you a marker of identification. Since your eyes are closed, you cannot see your body, and you cannot make a judgment as to how old you are. You could be fifteen, fifty, or seventy five years old. You have no idea of your location. It feels as if you could be anywhere. As the world knows it, you are lost. But this is as you truly are. This is where your peace lies. You are not the conditioning of your memories. You are not your body. You are all ages, because you are eternal. Those intervals of your life that have passed and those yet to come all exist in the present moment. And as the One, you are not located in one spot. You exist everywhere, and nowhere.

CHAPTER 10

A Puzzle

I have found my greatest joy and peace as I have recognized myself to be part of something much larger than what my perspective shows me. I am not special. My part is not grander than another's part, but neither is someone else's part more important than mine. I am not separate, and as I do my part, I am supported by those pieces around me who are doing their part. This book is a collaboration of numerous people fulfilling their parts so that we, as the Son, can remember. Timing is always perfect. When I am ready, the parts around me that will complete that experience will also be ready.

☥

What is it that we really want? To fit in. That doesn't mean to fit in socially. It means to know ourselves as part of a whole, to know that we have a purpose here. Don't we all want that?

This journey of God knowing Itself appears like a puzzle. The puzzle has always been complete, but it is the seeming appearance of pieces of the puzzle which defines God. Each of us, as an expression and manifestation of God, is a piece of the puzzle, and within each piece are more pieces and then more pieces, etc. There are no pieces which are better than others. There is no right or wrong way to put the puzzle together. When you go one way with reconstructing the puzzle, you have to put in certain pieces before other ones will fit. The *absence* of pieces defines the complete puzzle. This is how God, as all that exists, can know its Oneness, its wholeness. Joy comes with putting pieces into the puzzle, seeing the whole take shape. As pieces of the puzzle, we choose experiences which many would deem as "negative," but these experiences are simply the taking of pieces out so that they can be put back together. Rejoice and have gratitude in the awareness of this reconstruction process within yourself, because this is awareness of your divinity. When the puzzle is complete, we will do it all over again.

What happens if a piece of the puzzle is missing? Is the puzzle incomplete without the piece that is you? Every piece is essential to the whole puzzle. Not only is every piece needed to complete it, but every piece has the role of fitting in with the pieces around it. When we recognize this and we allow ourselves to be placed into our spot in the puzzle, we go into place without effort. The fit is perfect, and because of this, the seams between pieces become blurred. So much so that when we take a step back from the puzzle, we no longer see individual pieces. We see only the whole.

The puzzle is Love. There are no missing pieces, there is no separation. Yet, we pretend there are missing pieces. What do you have when Love appears missing? Fear, guilt, self judgment, shame, just to name a few. We get attached to a "negative" connotation around these, but when you put a piece of the puzzle back by remembering that Love was never not present, you simply acknowledge that self judgment or fear no longer serves the purpose for which it was used, which was to know your Oneness.

☥

CHAPTER 11

Power

There is a certain amount of power that a parent has over a child by the nature of their relationship, but when the parent crosses boundaries that should not be crossed, that power has been abused. My mother crossed the boundary and abused her power, and this made me very angry. I carried this anger into my relationships with my wife and kids, and when I raged, I felt powerful. Instead of going to the source of that anger, I was letting it seep out to those whom I loved the most and whom I wished to hurt the least. As I raged, I was unknowingly directing it at my mother. The sins of one generation being passed to the next. But when I raged, I wasn't powerful. I was very weak. Power comes from love. It does not come from hurting or victimizing someone else. Power comes from defenselessness, not defensiveness.

☥

You often hear the expression "the rich and powerful." The world assigns power based on position and wealth, but is this true power, for either of these can evaporate overnight. Surely, true power cannot be so variable.

True power is not variable, not changeable. True power does not come from something you take or something outside of yourself. It comes from your knowledge of your Oneness, the knowing that you are the dreamer of your dreams, the knowing that nothing is outside of you. True power is linked with taking responsibility. Every stone creates a ripple in the water. You are responsible for your actions, your words, your thoughts as well as your beliefs. If you see guilt in the world, it is because you see guilt within you, and only you can see the falsity of your beliefs. It is your dream. It is not reality. The effects of everything related to you act as ripples throughout the body of God. When you do not take responsibility, you deny who you are. Taking responsibility does not mean judging yourself or assigning blame, but it may mean something as simple as acknowledging when you say hurtful words and saying you are sorry. The simplest acts open Heaven's door. Taking responsibility is the recognition that there is the appearance of choice, and next time you might choose to create a different ripple pattern, one that is less disruptive to everything it encounters.

True power is never abused, never used for self interest or gain. There can be no judgment, no blame, when you know that our existence is neutral. Only the whole is seen, and with that comes the right use of power as well as the humility and desire to use this neutral energy in service to God.

You cannot find true power by giving it away. If you believe that someone, a spiritual teacher, the Pope, the garbage man, is closer to God than you, then you are giving away your power, the power that comes as the One. You labor under a false belief. Nothing can be substituted for your direct relationship with God. There is no one and no thing which can get you to "heaven" except your remembrance that you are already there. The only true and applicable remembrances of your Oneness are the remembrances that you have, not ones from someone else. Within this play we call Life, some may recognize their divinity sooner than others. Jesus only differed from everyone else in his recognition and remembrance. But you can remember in any instant, for you can only be what you are. Can a turtle be anything other than a turtle? When you are the turtle pretending to be a fox, it takes a lot of effort. Remembrance and recognition of what you are is effortless.

True power is a balance, a blending. The power of God is balanced with Her compassion and Love. Our society wants to assign power and a strong mind as a masculine quality, while feelings and an open heart are assigned to the feminine. But when you are in balance, your power is reflected and expressed through gentleness and love, whether you are male or female.

☥

CHAPTER 12

Experience

The experience that I had with my mother is fixed. By that I mean that an act occurred. A transfer of energy within the body of God happened. But how I view that act changes the experience. Early on, I viewed that experience with anger, grief, shame, and guilt. But as I revealed these hidden beliefs and emotions and I worked through them by bringing them to the Light, I saw the experience with my mother in a totally different way. Thought is creative and time is not fixed. There is only the one eternal moment, and everything is happening in that moment, all past and future experiences. Since there is only one moment, as I thought about my experience with my mother in a different light, I truly changed that experience. At times I wanted to go back and change what actually happened, but then I was getting caught up in the illusion. It was shown to me that the only true change occurs through thought, because that is the only creative vehicle in the Universe.

☥

Experience is the fulfillment of Creation. It is becoming that which we are. As a manifestation of God in form, everything you experience, God experiences. The deeper you are able to release into that truth, the deeper you know your Oneness. Is God's experience as an atheist different than God's experience through someone who fully knows their Oneness? It is different, but the experience is just as holy. The richness is in the appearance of differences, the infinite diversity of God in form. There are a small number of people who have chosen this experience to remember Absolute Truth, while there are others who have chosen this experience to not remember God at all. And many have chosen somewhere in between the two extremes. But all experiences are holy. If you see one experience as better than another, you are reverting back to a belief system of good and bad.

What is it you want from this experience? What is it you pray for? The most effective prayers are unspoken ones from the heart. Often when we pray with words, we are praying for a *better* experience. Think about most of the prayers that are said in the world. There is prayer for prosperity, wisdom, the health of someone, anything. These are all well intentioned, but by wanting one thing, we raise it to a higher level than its counterpart. We judge that being financially secure is better than being poor. We judge that a person should recover from a serious illness. These are only appearances. As God's expression, the joy is in just being able to have the experience.

Have you ever been awestruck at how the wind feels on your face or the smell of your favorite meal? If so, you have witnessed the holiness of having an experience in a body, the temple where God resides. However, your experience is not isolated to a body, because you are One. Since there is no separation, each manifestation or aspect of the body of God has a common experience with the other manifestations. When you have an experience, every human being shares in that. Similarly, you share in the experience of every human being, every animal, every tree, every mountain, every river, the clouds, the sun, the moon. Because of our Oneness, comparisons become meaningless. As waves in the ocean, we are all moved by the same tide or the same current. The beauty lies in the uniqueness of each wave.

Just as there is no separation across the One, there is no permanency to time. Only the one eternal moment exists, and it contains all "past" experiences as well as all "future" possibilities. As the One, you share in all experiences within this moment, whether it happened to the manifestation which is you or to another manifestation of God. Any "past" experience can be recalled and experienced in the Now. And because you exist only in the Now, any "past" experience can be changed, simply by realizing it exists only in this moment and thinking different of it. Through His thought, God created each of us as an extension of Himself. Thought is the creative vehicle of the universe, and as co-creators, through our thought, we have the ability to change any experience.

☥

CHAPTER 13

Thought

Thought can seem like the biggest impediment to "progress," and it can also be the door which opens Heaven. For me it has been both. I have witnessed or been aware of my thoughts for a long time, yet at times the form and the content of my thoughts was one of heavy self judgment, causing me great frustration and concern. As I have climbed the mountain, I have more frequently recognized through the contrast that these thoughts were Love, and that they appeared to help me see that I am also Love. I often struggled with not falling into the trap of seeing two types of thought, that is thought from a localized mind some would call an ego, versus thought from my higher or God self. For a good part of my journey, it appeared that there were two types of thought and that I was switching back and forth, but this is another paradox.

☥

There are not two types of thought. There is only the appearance of two types. All thought is held within the One. The localized mind believes that it is all that exists, that it is not part of a greater whole. We are familiar with its thought system, because we have each lived with that system throughout our lives. But what is thought as it relates to God?

THOUGHT

As it relates to God, each of us, as the Sonship, represents a differentiating thought in the Mind of God, providing the contrast for God to know Itself. God created us from his Word, from thought, and that is who we are, notwithstanding the appearance of a physical body. We exist only as a Love thought, and God "thinks" of each of us without ceasing, otherwise we would cease to "exist." Just as a thought can never leave your mind, you can never leave, never be separate, from your Source.

Because God's thought is formless, there is only the appearance of physical reality. If you were able to fully live this Truth and your Oneness, you would be able to manipulate "reality," just as Jesus multiplied the loaves and the fish. You are the actor, the director, the producer, the writer—anything can happen and you can manifest anything that you choose. And you would be able to move in and out of this world at will.

Thought cannot change the changeless. The one eternal moment, the moment of our creation, is as it has always been. One God, eternal, unmoved. Our separation or fall in consciousness, and our return in consciousness, are complete. Once God thought it, it was complete. Only the illusion of time gives the appearance that choices can be made as to which path we take in our return and the appearance that we can delay or accelerate the return.

☥

CHAPTER 14

Meaning of Life

Although I probably did not realize it at that time, my wanting to know the meaning of life and why I exist was what propelled me on a search. Like the large majority of people on this planet, until my thirties I went through the motions of life, never probing deeper and asking why. That anyone would not ask this question seems almost incomprehensible to me now, but until the River of Life brings that push, that hardship, that calamity, each of us walks through the world asleep. I think my push was the desire to be the best husband and father that I could. As I gradually awakened, I still struggled with meaning --- why, why, why. But at some point I stopped asking questions and I knew the meaning was a part of me. I was the answer to the questions I had been seeking.

☥

The meaning of life is simple. It is what you make of it. Sure, we are here for Love to know Itself, but Love can know Itself regardless of whether each of us recognizes this process going on or not. To put it another way, Love is having an experience of Itself, but only a small number of people are aware of that. For them, as it has been for me, that is the meaning of life. Rather, that is what gives life meaning. My exploration of this process and my journey of self discovery have taken importance for me. For others what is important is totally different. For a long time I thought that everyone wanted this path. How could they not since God is all there is and Divine Love is beyond description. But I came to see that this is an arrogant view not borne from the Mind of God. While the One is all there is, it is not all that has meaning within the context of God taking form. And without the form, Love could not know Itself. I have come to recognize that we each need to meet others where they are, for this has meaning to the other person and this creates meaning between the two people. The mirrors must be aligned exactly across from each other to create the reflection.

So we can say that life has no meaning except what an individual assigns to it. Because each individual assigns a different meaning, there is no absolute. And that is the ultimate freedom which allows us to discover and live as the Love that we are. When we know that we are only Love, we are completely free and our innate joy blooms. We can laugh at ourselves and the circumstances that Life presents to us, and we can laugh at what had been our reaction to getting too caught up in something that was not real. We can enjoy the *appearance* of differences, just as a child enjoys playing pretend for fun and pure joy.

Since there are no absolutes as related to meaning, we can step back and see this existence as a dream, similar to a play in which we are all actors. Our role and the overall play only have meaning to the extent that being in an actual play has meaning. And the play will end. Heaven and Earth shall pass away. No one should get too upset or judge anything that happens within the play. When you do, just remember it is your "play mind" which believes that what is happening is something other than a play, which is all it can do, because the "play mind" only exists in the play.

In summary, it takes the *appearance* of meaning to give meaning. Only through the contrast and paradox created by the appearance can God know Itself.

☥

CHAPTER 15

What is Real

Recognition of my Real self was the easy part. There was nothing I could do to "make" this self appear. It came when I was ready through the grace of God. For me, there was a huge contrast to the self I had known and which I had identified with. Whereas I had lived in fear, my Real self knows only peace and joy. As my illusory self saw separation, my Real self lives in Oneness and communion with God. Where my old self was constantly living in and worried about the future, my true self knows only the present moment. The hard part for me has always been the "loss" of that Real self, those times when I spiraled back into identifying fully or at least partially with that old self. This was one of the most difficult and one of the most frustrating parts of the spiritual journey. Of course, I could never lose this self. It only appeared that I could lose it.

☥

Each of us can rejoice, for what is Real is permanent. It can never be changed, never affected by anything. Do you direct your attention, your consciousness, to what is Real or what is not real? Experiences come and go, but what is Real can never be taken away. You can rejoice, for what is Real is you.

This you is not the you who makes appearances in the world. Your concept of self is not your Self. You are not the role you play, not the doctor, not the high level business manager, not the movie star. You are not the parent of a great athlete or a gifted student, not the middle child, not the forgotten grandparent. You are not the recovering alcoholic, not the abuser, and you are not the victim. These are all identities that you want to cling to out of fear, but these identities come and go, just like the scenery on the River of Life. It is not who you *think* you are. It is who you are.

There is a tremendous release that comes with being the Real you. When you realize that you no longer have to pretend to be something that you are not, you feel the immense freedom to live as the true essence of your Being, and you are very grateful. No longer is it necessary to think about whom you are and how you operate in the world. Nor is it necessary to plan neither your "attack" of another person nor your defense of the attack you perceive from them. All of the illusions, all of the games, fall away. Nothing is required of you, and there is in fact nothing you can do, because God moves through your very Being. Everything slows down for you and becomes clear, because in order to keep up the illusion, you had been moving at a frantic pace. You are Real, not contrived. You are authentic. It takes no effort to be who you really are.

As part of being who you really are, you lose the seriousness. Why have all of the saints, prophets, and mystics laughed so much? When you were a child, did you enjoy playing games, playing pretend? Did you take any of it as serious?

This is a process of elimination. You eliminate all that isn't. What are you left with? That which is Real. You continue to see differences, but no longer do you "live" in them, always looking for the better. When you no longer see and believe in differences, you can enjoy the appearance of differences while knowing they are not real.

How can you see what is Real by what is not real? Love appears in all forms. Even your beliefs, thoughts, and actions which you deem negative show you overwhelming Love. It is only through them, through their Love, that you can see what is Real. Because they are Love which is appearing in a form which is not Real, simply through their demonstration, you see what is Real.

CHAPTER 16

The Good Stuff
Fear, Anger, Self Judgment, Guilt, and Shame

I came to intimately know the above states. When they arrived, they came bearing gifts of Love, although I certainly did not feel that way when I was experiencing them. My journey has been one where guilt, self judgment, and especially anger and fear have risen to a conscious level in me literally hundreds of times. Each time they have arisen, I have seen them with a slightly different perspective, since I have been in a different place each time. I have used various strategies to deal with them. Especially with fear: I have fought it, tried to rationalize it away, ignored it, embraced it, and seen it as Love. All of these strategies worked, and none worked, even simultaneously. That was the paradox which presented itself to me as it related to growing emotionally and spiritually. While I took a higher perspective, I also allowed these energies, such as anger or fear, to be processed when they arose within me, especially if they related to emotional traumas that my body was holding on to. I spiraled back and forth from the higher perspective to one where I *felt as if the emotion had overtaken me. It was hard to deal with this back and forth, but this is actually a good sign. On my journey I feel as if I paid far too much attention to the fear, believing that I could do **something** to get me through it. That was a false belief.*

☥

Grief, anger, fear, shame, guilt. Regardless of whether someone recognizes themselves as being on a path, everyone must deal with these energies. Yet, these are all the same energy, the only energy that exists: Love. When we see the above as anything other than just energy, when we see them as bad or different, they become obstructed and stuck in us. Only the expression of the energy, not the energy itself, is different, and that is where the beauty and holiness lie. If we dread having to express the grief or anger, and if we believe that the "good stuff" is on the other side after we get rid of all of the grief, etc., we miss the whole point. The grief, the anger, the fear, these *are* the good stuff. Only the good stuff exists. Only God exists.

Thus these things that we run from—self judgment, guilt, fear—are no different than any part of the One. They are Love, a gift to help us better see who we really are. They are a gift from God, of Herself, to Herself.

When these energies arise in your mind, neither move toward them nor pull away from them. When we withdraw the belief they are separate and no longer make judgment on them, the energy returns to its undifferentiated state. The wave releases its form back into the ocean.

The paradox is that while these energies are present and are uncomfortable, they actually do not exist in the form that is making them uncomfortable. If we recognize that we have guilt, fear, and judgment to give up, then we are still within the illusion. The illusion is that we have *anything* to give up. We are complete as we are. Guilt, fear, and judgment do not exist in the form that they appear. How can we give up something that does not exist?

Of all of these, fear may be the most precious gift, for it may be the greatest teacher.

Fear arises from seeing apparent differences and *believing* them. That is how we "fell from grace." We believed in differences, and we judged them. We judged our self guilty, and we saw our self as separate, no longer One with Grace. But what if we could live a reality of Truth, where we see and enjoy the appearance of differences while knowing that they are not real and that there is only the One.

Because of the appearance of fear, we try to drive it away, deny its existence, or go through it to get to something *better* on the other side. All of these deny the reality that we are One with it, just as we are with everything else. Fear does not exist, because it is Love in costume. But try telling that to someone who is fearful of death, or someone who is fearful, as was the case with me, of being annihilated in God's Love. When fear appears real to us, as in these situations and many more, it leads to contraction, which seems to confirm and magnify the appearance of fear. How do we get out of this? Again, it is an illusion to believe that we need to give up or get out of anything. Just be who you are---Love. Love is expansiveness, not contraction. Love gives of itself, wholly and unconditionally. By being what you are, you remember and know yourself only as you are. All else does not exist.

Fear can also lead us into false beliefs. One such belief is if it is present, there must be separation from God. But it is the other way around. Fear feels like fear, it feels crummy, because you first believe that you are separate. Fear follows the belief in separation, but then is falsely used to confirm the belief. This is the dog chasing his tail scenario. Also, because we are One, there is no state that is you alone. Whatever you are feeling or experiencing, whether it be guilt, fear, or joy, cannot be finite and particular to you alone. The worse guilt or fear feels, the more you are identifying as a separate "me." The peace of God can only be known when you walk as the Oneness, no separation, no differences.

The greater one identifies with fear, the more one thinks they have the answers. The greater one identifies with fear, the more one sees fear in the world. The greater one identifies with fear, the more one attributes this to God, as God is seen not as Love, but as a punishing Father.

Anger is the best indicator that fear is present, because all anger, where our words and thoughts do not match our true state of

Being, originates from fear, no matter the circumstance. If you can get behind the anger to see the fear, it will take many forms---fear of being poor, fear of growing old, fear of death. But these are only appearances. What is the fear that is central to all minds? All forms of fear flow from the one fear of uncovering a belief that you have about yourself, a belief that you see as so hideous that you would do whatever it takes to keep this belief hidden. The appearance of evil in this world is an attempt, individually and collectively, to project this hatred and this truth away from the believer so that it remains hidden. This belief, which goes hand in hand with the illusion of sacrifice, is that you are deserving of the most awful death because of the "sins" you have committed against God, especially the sin of separation. And in order for God not to see these sins, you have chosen yourself as the judge, jury, and executioner. This is an extremely strong belief that is central to how we operate and to our illusion of thought within this world, and all other beliefs, like, I am not worthy, etc. are this central belief appearing in a different form. Only a handful of individuals in the history of the world have broken clear of this belief. Anytime we anger, we are touching on this belief. But your anger and fear are Love, Love that will show you the falsity of your belief that sin exists and that you could ever do any harm against God.

If only the One exists, when you have fear, you are fearful of yourself. How can that be? Bingo.

Self judgment is an offshoot of fear. Those who have the strongest egos actually feel the least confident about themselves. They have the greatest self judgment, although they have hidden it well from themselves. But you are only the attributes of God, the attributes of the One. Self judgment is not one of them. When you walk as the One, even the concept of self judgment does not exist, for it is an illusion.

As described earlier in the book, judgment and self judgment are the same. Jesus taught the world about judgment, but his words have been misinterpreted. Jesus was not admonishing us not to judge. If we have not released our belief system of right and wrong, then when we judge, we see that as wrong, and we judge our judgment. Judgment is not separate from the One. Jesus was telling us that if we live in recognition of our Oneness, then judgment is not present.

As described above, guilt (with its accompanying shame) over the belief that you have sinned against God, goes hand in hand with fear. Guilt is very recognizable in the world, and many believe that they are truly guilty because they see themselves as guilty. You appear to yourself as you see yourself. If you see yourself as guilty, then it appears to you as though you are truly guilty. Appearances seem to become real. Then when you know yourself to be guilty, the "evidence" for your belief is provided. But you are as God created you, as is all Creation, inseparable from your Source, wholly neutral, neither positive nor negative.

Guilt within the world operates on "shoulds," but there are no "shoulds." Should implies that if you don't do something, you are guilty, and guilt is what obscures our Oneness, our holiness. There are no good or bad choices. As we float on the River of Life, we do not choose what the River brings to us. We float by something, and that is how we choose what is applicable and what we pursue at that point in our life.

So if everything is Love, then why does Love take on the appearance of guilt or of fear? To show you, through contrast, that it *is* Love. Extreme guilt or fear can be one of the greatest teachers of your Life. Large rocks that are exposed in the river define the river. The rocks are still part of the river, but the current flows unimpeded over and around the rocks, and eventually the water completely erodes the rocks away. The guilt, the fear, the self judgment, they all allow you to go to the depths in your recognition. Without guilt as the contrast, innocence cannot be known. Everything serves a purpose. Everything serves the purpose of showing you that you are Love. When you rest in that Love and your deep Longing for God, self judgment, fear, guilt, and anger all disappear, for they were never there.

With any of these energies, when they no longer serve you, you drop them without emotion, without attachment. This is anything which causes a reaction in you. The reaction was there to help you, especially if it is one of anger. Anger at God not only is okay, it is almost a prerequisite to moving through at times. But when it is no longer needed, you can bless it for its Love and let it go. The same is true for fear, guilt, shame or self judgment.

God is. God is acceptance of what is, including the appearance of guilt, fear, anger, etc. When you feel separate because of guilt pertaining to your "sins" against God, and you let that be what it is, you surrender to the paradox of accepting and not trying to change or flee the very thing which creates the feeling of separation. When you are fully able to stay in that paradox, then the energy that took the appearance of guilt will no longer appear in that form. As with all states in the One, embrace the totality of your being. That means all thoughts, all judgments, all emotions, all beliefs, all fears, all love, all joy, and all peace. Is your shame, your guilt, not Him? How about your lust, your resentment, your hatred? Your grief, your pain? Is your self judgment not Him? We cannot drive Him away from Himself.

☥

CHAPTER 17

The One

As I increasingly came to see my Oneness, it brought up questions that were initially disconcerting. I am part of the greater whole, but how do I now fit in to the groups I have been associated with? How do I see myself in relation to my siblings, to my wife, my kids? Am I just an actor in a play, or am I part of a larger soul group which has come together? How do I relate to friends who knew me before I began this journey?

☥

God is One. Have you ever thought about what this means? It is not the same as saying there is one God. The closest analogy would be to say that God is complete, or that God is whole. God is One means that nothing exists outside of God, nothing exists outside of Itself. Everything serves a purpose. Every piece of the puzzle is necessary for completion. The way the sun rises, the path the bird flies across the sky, the sound a gun makes, the thoughts and experiences you have, and the actions you take. All are intricate to the whole, regardless of how "minor" they seem. The One exists in the present and only, eternal moment. That is inescapable joyous truth.

On my journey I have found that Life is the greatest awakener and teacher of this Oneness that there is. Sometimes I have not immediately appreciated (somewhat resisted) the lessons I was being shown, but I have eventually seen each of them as the Love that they are, and I have been grateful for each one. If you will be completely open, you will see the lessons in an infinite number of Life forms. Life may be represented by a human being who has walked before you and is consciously aware of their Oneness. Sometimes it might mean a human being who has no awareness. It might be an animal, or the way the cloud moves across the sky. Life is your anger, your stillness, your thoughts, your experiences. The desire for a red convertible, or the way you talk to God. All of these are Life. Everything, every object, every action, every emotion, every circumstance you encounter, everything shows you, with extreme gentleness, compassion, and Love, your Oneness.

As we live the Oneness, we see that it is like a continuum. We want to separate Life into black and white. We want to describe ourselves as healthy, joyful, or guilty, but we are not a point on the continuum. We are the whole continuum, and the continuum is Stillness. Just as the ocean is never at rest, we are constantly moving up and down the continuum. This apparent movement creates our existence by giving definition and contrast to the Stillness.

Like the tree which has roots extending into the ground and branches extending into the sky, God is the one trunk from which all his creations flow. Just like the roots and branches, Heaven and Earth are One. Oneness has no separation.

Why are we not aware of the Oneness, of God's presence being closer than our breath? We are not aware of Her, because we deny a part of ourselves. We judge what we are, what we do, what we think. Simply believing that one of our thoughts is bad is enough to block our awareness of God expressing as us, through us. God is All, and She is all experiences. To say that one experience or one thought is better than another is to say that God is not One, that God can be divided. When we no longer judge anything that arises in us and through us, then Her presence is constant.

As you recognize this Oneness with God, you also recognize the Oneness, the wholeness within yourself. For what is transpiring within you is a microcosm, a reflection of what is transpiring in the complete body of God. This means the recognition of those parts of yourself that you have attempted to hide in the shadows because of beliefs you have surrounding those parts. You have "separated" from those parts, attempting to leave them behind as you put a brave face to the world, looking outside yourself. Yet, you can never leave them behind. These parts of you are frozen in time, often related to childhood emotional traumas and blockages. It as if the river is frozen and unable to flow and give its sustenance to the rest of you. You have fear around the Light uncovering these parts, because you feel guilt over "leaving" them behind, and you may feel guilt over something related to the original reason for the blockage. But as with everything else, your beliefs are false, and your overwhelming Love for these parts will finally show you this. These parts await your return to yourself. They await your retrieval of them, because their desire to be whole is as strong as yours. You are the re-claimer of these parts as well as the re-claimee, and you are also the clear vessel through which God's Love takes form, enabling the reclamation to take place. There is no blame by these parts. There is only Love. When you come home to God, you come home to yourself.

When you accept others exactly as they are, you are recognizing the Oneness, and you are accepting yourself as you are. And since the body of God is neutral, there is no separation. Anything that *appears* done to you is done by you. Since there is nothing outside of you, the idea of blame is meaningless.

As we enter a time of new consciousness, everything undertaken must be done with pure intent, or it will not be successful. The intent must not be for the individual; it must be for the glory of God and the whole. We must begin to see how we live in a world which reflects separation, not Oneness. One of the most difficult aspects of existing in this world and especially this society is that there are artificially created differences which don't exist. There is the weekday and the weekend. Some like the weekday because they prefer working over leisure time. For others it is the opposite, and the clash between the two desires accentuates the difference. We celebrate the holidays of Thanksgiving and Christmas, when guilt and unconscious expectations around family run rampant, along with expectations about how we *should* feel. We can be grateful every day of our life, and we can celebrate the birth of the Christ within us every day. These artificially created differences do not exist. Without your being lost in them, you can be present every moment of every day. The sun rises every day, and the birds chirp and fly every day. They do not know any difference. Nothing real changes when it becomes the weekend or Christmas day.

As the appearance of the world moves into alignment with Oneness, each of us will also reflect this within ourselves, for we are the One. Complete peace and freedom will be the states in which you reside, for these are inherent in the One. Belief will fade away, because there is no need to believe in Truth. It is self evident. Only God will remain, and in each moment your eyes will look with wonder and gratitude upon Creation.

CHAPTER 18

Understanding

As I look back to my childhood, I realize that I was never comfortable in who I was. Part of this was attributable to the trauma inflicted by my mother, but part of this was the fact that I had a hard time adjusting to this world. I came from a space of infinite Allness to one where I was limited. I mentioned in an earlier chapter about the brick wall and the inability to understand an infinite Universe. My mind, which was very logical and analytical, could not grasp this "other world." When the mind cannot understand something, it will fear it. This is especially true of the mind understanding God. When my mind became fearful of the unknown, it attempted to become even stronger, blocking out any memory of my true nature.

☥

This journey cannot be understood. The sooner you accept that, the sooner you will be at peace. Understanding is a natural seeking for the mind. For a long time I tried to understand what was happening for me on this path and where I was headed. But my understanding never took me there, and it won't for you either. God happens. It is not that you think it and then you go there. Trying to understand is a form of control that comes from fear.

Clarity requires something being finite, but God is not finite. Allow the River of Life to take you in the direction it presents. Just as the waters swirl in the river, constantly moving you along with changing scenery, there is a steady stream of thoughts, emotions, and experiences that swirl into you and back out of you. Just like the boat trip on the river, you simply enjoy the ride. You don't have to know (clarity) where you are going or even where you are at in that moment. Fear, as in clinging to a rock or wanting to stop the boat, arises from wanting to know where you are at and not being *able* to know.

Non-understanding is the state of *Being*, not a state of doing or thinking. When you reside in non-understanding, you are present in the body, not the mind. This state helps you let go of the rock in the River, so that the River can carry you without your resistance.

When you see that you really don't know or understand anything, then you are free to Be. You submit to the wisdom of the body of God, allowing the River of Life to reveal Itself to you. In the world, learning operates under the belief that something can be known and understood. How can we know something which is Infinite? How can an individual tree know how far the forest extends?

God cannot know Himself as Love without appearing to be separate parts, without appearing to be something. But even these parts cannot be understood, because they are forms which are in constant change, never stationary or fixed.

Acceptance that you cannot understand anything leads to great humility and a joyous opening and softening of the heart. When the heart is open, all judgment passes away, and God is able to reveal Himself to you. The eyes see with a gentleness and a compassion that expresses the Love that we are. Freedom is yours, and you are open to all possibilities. And God is infinite possibilities.

The paradox is that while we do not understand anything, we know the Truth of our Being. We know ourselves as Love, as the One.

Trust in the unknown. That is all that is "known," all that is certain, all that can be counted on. God is infinite, unlimited possibilities. When we trust in the unknown, we trust in God.

☥

CHAPTER 19

Our Purpose

My purpose is something that I struggled with extensively, for I was trying to understand. As demonstrated in the last chapter, this is impossible. My ego, out of fear, created all of these grand notions. But when all of that static died away, I was able to see my purpose in the simplest things in life. My children's laughs, their smiles, and their pure joy in living, spurred my remembrance and showed me where I wanted to go <u>back</u> to. And I knew that I would do anything, go through any pain, to get there. The world would be a totally different place if we all lived from that joy.

☥

We are here to be happy. That is not a requirement, for there are no requirements. God asks nothing of us, for he lives through our Being, giving us total freedom, which is why we *are* happy. To put it another way, why would God place a burden or requirement on Himself? So how can you be happy? Be who you are.

You are not here to *do* anything. You are here to *be*. You are fulfilling your role on Earth just by being an expression of God in form, for this is Creation fulfilled. This is Love. When you are what you are, there is tremendous joy, an intrinsic happiness. While you are not here to do anything, you can still enjoy your role in this illusion, just as an actor enjoys his part in a play. How do you find your part in the play of Life? Follow your joy, and let God do the rest.

Although there is nothing we must do, each of us fills a unique purpose. Our role in the body of God parallels our physical body. Each organ, each cell, has a specialized role or function, just as each of us has a specialized function and purpose within the body of God. The body cannot operate, cannot live, without each part doing its function. Each cell in our body is complete and whole in and of itself, a miniature version of the body of God. A duplicate, and yet at the same time, it is the whole. The two cannot be separate. Where does a drop of water in the ocean begin and end? Every cell, every atom, appears individual, yet each has its own consciousness and knows itself as the One. Our physical bodies serve as an aid and constant reminder that we appear separate but are One.

You are fulfilling your role by *Being*. We live in a world that values doing and thinking instead of being, which is our natural state. Thinking is outside the present moment, revolving around something in the "past" or something in the "future." Thinking requires effort. As we simply are in the present moment, the River of Life just carries us along without any effort on our part. When we release any beliefs or judgments about the past and any preconceived notions about the future, the past and the future become what they are, the present moment. And in that moment the River of Life gently carries us along, providing all that we could ever need. Rejoice in this Truth, and be happy in your *Being*.

CHAPTER 20

The Spiritual Journey

For the past fifteen years, I have been on what many would describe as a spiritual journey. With the benefit of hindsight, I know this period is actually longer, encompassing my whole life, but my recognition of a journey dates back to this time. These fifteen years have included many peak experiences as well as many periods in the valley. This time also consisted of a lot of searching and questing, looking for God "in all the wrong places." The River of Life brought me numerous spiritual books, extensive emotional therapy, vision quests, spiritual helpers, and much more. All of these forms were fine at the time, as they spurred my remembrance, but I was consumed with finding what I thought was missing instead of looking at what was there. There was no need to look further than myself. I discovered that the universe was contained within me in the one holy moment in which I existed, and the spiritual journey was present in every form, not just those forms with which I had been obsessed.

☥

The word journey is a misnomer. How can we be on a journey somewhere when we are already there? We already rest in perfection and wholeness. Therein lays the paradox. What is called the spiritual journey is both the easiest and hardest thing you will do. It is the easiest, because you are already that perfect diamond, beautiful beyond description and infinite in clarity. How easy it is to be what you are! It is the hardest, because you believe that the diamond is misshapen and needs to be polished and that your salvation depends on this. You ask for God's help in arranging for the diamond to be reshaped and polished. It takes a very hard surface to reshape a diamond.

Is someone more spiritual than another? You are an expression of God, as is everyone else. God chooses to express and know Himself in an infinite number of ways. If within this play of Life you are an expression that remembers your Oneness more than another person, this "spiritual advancement" is not better or worse, because the joy is just in being able to have the experience. Some of you are like the hair on the body of God, while others are the toes, or the organs. All parts serve their purpose in the body. As remembrance unfolds, some of you lead the way, while others follow, and others drag their feet. All can't lead the way, but leading the way is not "better" than dragging your feet. All ways are needed to create the contrast for God to be able to have the experience of Himself. All parts are needed to function as a whole. If you judge another person's experience, then you are forgetting that God is expressing as that person, and you are also forgetting that God is expressing as you.

The error in seeing yourself on a spiritual path is that you believe someone can be on the path while someone else is not. There is no path. There is only the One, and that energy can be expressed in an infinite number of ways. In order to support its belief in its own existence, the mind makes an impossible attempt to fit the infinite expression of the One into a box labeled spiritual. If spiritual is defined as being, within the illusion of time, on a journey of remembrance back to recognition of our Oneness, then everything is spiritual, regardless of whether a person recognizes that they are on the journey.

If you believe that on this path you have somewhere to go or something to attain, you will always have somewhere to go or something to attain. You believe in a search which does not exist. Within the illusion of time, belief always delays your recognition of your Oneness. The belief that you can do something to help move yourself faster along this path is actually what impedes your progress. Of yourself, you are nothing.

Now, the other side of the paradox is that we live in a time and space based world where we are advancing in our recognition and remembrance and there is the appearance of a journey. There are certain practices (such as reading this book) which will cultivate this remembrance, and the River of Life will present those to you that are appropriate at that time. As the River presents different scenery to you, you may only identify part of it as the journey, but everything is the journey back to remembrance of your Oneness. As you encounter a particular item on the River, do not assume that this is what you will always see or that a certain ritual or a certain interest will be the way it always is for you. As the River continually flows, we move up and down the continuum that constitutes our Being.

We "see" and are attracted to certain scenery or certain points along the continuum, but the flow continues, carrying us to the next thing we "see." That flow is God.

When you are no longer drawn toward something on the continuum and it becomes dry or rote for you, then release it. This applies to any statement in this book, any practice or ritual, an exercise routine, a job, a daily walk, a prayer or set of affirmations, anything. God will always provide something to make our heart sing with joy. If we resist and try to stay with something that no longer makes our heart sing, the scenery along the River of Life becomes boring, and the current smashes us against the rock we try to hold on to out of fear. Be completely open to wherever the River takes you, and be completely honest with yourself as to whether you are clinging to a rock for fear of moving deeper into your Self.

Yes, there may be certain practices that you do or certain prayers that you say which help you feel more connected with God and Her Presence, but if you become attached to these, you are seeing differences and creating a separation which does not exist. Life is a walking, breathing, meditative Love affair with the Divine. God is present in the simplest of activities, the wildest of thoughts, the lowest and highest of emotions. He is present in your fingernail, the Grand Canyon, the bricks in your house. He is present whether you never do yoga, meditate, or pray again. Yes, do those activities or say those affirmations if you feel led to do so. If you don't, don't. It will not change anything. There can be no change to the One. The valley and the mountain are the same. You can heal someone of cancer, or you can go to the bathroom. It is all the same. It is Love.

Only within the illusion of time can you delay recognition of your Oneness. You are like a huge cruise ship which has a southern destination. Each and every moment, God gives you Life hints to help you remember to go south. He may even provide a tugboat. But out of fear, some of us go north. When you initially move north, the ship is moving at a slow speed and can easily be turned around. But if you keep moving north, you get farther and farther away from your "destination," and at full speed the ship takes a while to turn around. If you don't want to go north, then follow those Life hints which will awaken your remembrance, but be completely honest with yourself. If you are only playing with spiritual toys, then you are delaying your recognition, similar to someone who is a workaholic or someone who uses drugs and alcohol or the computer to cover their fear of going south. The word spiritual defines an illusory grouping that is just another form for the appearance of Love. It is not Love Itself. Without the illusion of time and space, north and south become the same, and all "choices" are seen as leading to God. We are all headed "south." Knowing this, how could we ever judge our own or someone else's choices?

Do we need a spiritual teacher? Everyone must learn to rely on inner guidance, but there are times when outside help is warranted. This could come in the form of a person, an animal, or a book. Anything can fill this role, for all is One. If the guide is a person, there are certain qualifications that a true teacher will have. A true teacher adds nothing but rather helps you take away that which you think exists but does not. He or she is not attached in any way to being a teacher, nor are they attached to any outcome for an individual whom has received their teachings. A true teacher knows that words are only symbols for the unfathomable, and they convey their message in as few words as possible, demonstrating that God is simplicity and that Love is all that exists. He or she knows that they are both the teacher and the student, because they teach to themselves, as the act of giving and receiving are the same. As a reflection of God, they are in complete balance. Power and thought (the Father) are balanced with extreme gentleness, compassion, and Love (the Divine Mother). How do you find such a person? If such a person exists for you, God will take care of the details. But if you are waiting, you will miss listening to your own inner voice, and you will miss all of the teachers whom you encounter in your daily interactions.

Why is the search for God and for answers important? There is no search because what you seek is within you. But within the illusion of time, we are strongly driven at times to search for answers, to search for the return to God and Love, because it is the contrast to the act of searching that finally shows us there is nothing outside ourselves and that the search does not exist.

Similarly, we can see that the journey is like a seesaw or a rocking back and forth. While we are never separate from God, sometimes we have to feel separate. We spiral down into those areas which need further work on integration and in doing so this provides the contrast so that we can know our Oneness at a deeper level the next time. When you feel the farthest away from God, the contrast with being "there" is huge. Although you are not "there," you are very aware of "there" due to the contrast, and "there" becomes very pronounced.

The spiral of the journey is similar to the funnel of a tornado or one which is formed as water goes down a drain. At the top the spiral is much wider, and the "time" between one side of the spiral and the other, between those "connected" and "non-connected" states, is measured in decades, even longer. As you move down the spiral, the rotation increases, and you encounter the change in states more quickly. In addition, you also move down the spiral in an increasingly faster pace, until eventually, you reach the bottom of the spiral, where you enter the black hole of nothingness, one devoid of states and change---the Oneness.

If horrific thoughts arise within us or we judge ourselves harshly, have we fallen off our spiritual center? The question has no meaning. There is no off/on. There is no spiritual/non-spiritual, no compassionate/non-compassionate.

Patience.

How does fear play into the journey? Since you are in a bodily form which is based under the illusion of time and space, fear is inevitable. It is present in your cells. It is present, to a large degree, in the world. Some will have to deal with it more than others, and it will come and go within your journey. There is one transitional time on the journey when you feel considerable fear as well as feeling His Presence constantly with you. This is a time when your belief in separation is frequently exposed to the Light and its Truth, when you alternate between being asleep and remaining awake with new vision. It is a time when you remember that you are not separate and that fear is not what you are. His Presence can be felt in every moment, because that is what you are. As you listen to His Voice and follow His Will more frequently, your life runs with the ease of a hot knife slicing through butter. Circumstances which you had previously viewed as negative no longer appear to you as rocks in the River. The River is seamless.

During this transitional time and at other times on the journey, there are many instances when you need to be still and alone for extended periods of time. Equally important are the periods when you must be part of the world, interacting with other expressions of God. For in order for God to help you remember who you really are, there must be opportunities presented where you can practice, and this cannot be done if you isolate yourself. Remember those people and situations where you have become the angriest? Those are some of the greatest opportunities.

The bottom line is that everyone alive, regardless of whether they recognize a journey, is undergoing change. Expansion and contraction, and the corresponding death and rebirth, are the natural cycles of the universe, from our cells and our breath to the economy and the environment. Individually and collectively we have attempted to alter the natural cycle by pushing expansions indefinitely and by shortening contractions, but this cannot be done. If the expansion is pushed artificially, the corresponding contraction is that much quicker and more severe in order to achieve balance. Contraction is necessary to create the contrast to the expansion. The appearance of change is inevitable. If we resist contraction, if we resist change, the change will be appear in a form that is more severe. The change will come in the form of a hurricane, figuratively and literally, which restores the natural balance by violently washing everything out to sea, as opposed to the tide, which is slow and gentle. Love is slow and gentle, if you don't resist the change.

Eventually you reach the bridge which spans heaven and Earth. As you step onto the bridge, you come to a full recognition that there is no turning back. There never was. You just didn't recognize it until now. This recognition gives you both peace and fear. Peace, because you know that you are fully in the hands of God. Fear, because you can no longer operate under the illusion that you have any control. You go wherever the River takes you. Do you have faith that whatever happens is a demonstration of God's immense Love for you? Does this mean that you could be financially destitute or that you could suffer ill health? By this time you no longer fear your own death, but could it mean the death of a loved one? Appearances can take many forms. Only God's Love for you and your Love for Her is Real.

☥

CHAPTER 21

A Poem

☥

The call of Life stirs the soul,
Bringing wonder to every moment.
Who but God knows the answer?
It is found in the wind and the trees,
And it dies to every whisper.
But Behold, thou knowest,
Thou sayest, in all his Glory.

CHAPTER 22

Illusion and Truth

For a long time on the journey, I used illusion as a crutch to sometimes not do life. As an answer to a problem, I would sometimes tell my wife and kids that it is all an illusion, so what use is there in being part of the world, in taking responsibility. This was my ego trying to use spiritual truth for its own means and survival. I am an actor in a play, but I still need to give all of my energy to my role even though I know it is not real. In this dream that I am experiencing, I must fully do life while at the same time carrying the knowing that it is all an illusion. Knowing this still did not prevent me from getting caught up in the game, in the web of the illusion. I was like an insect that wanted to go to the Light but had to fly through the spider's web to get there, and I continued getting caught in the web, suffering as the host of the web devoured me. I continued like this until I saw that the Light is in me, thus there is nowhere to go. Then magically, somehow the web disappears.

☥

One could describe illusion as the opposite of Truth. Yet Truth has no opposite. Truth is. It encompasses everything without end. However, without the appearance of illusion providing the contrast, Truth could not be revealed.

If you feel caught in the web, covered up with illusion, do not fight it. Do not analyze it, break it down, justify it, or place it in some hierarchy. The form it takes is irrelevant. Simply recognize Truth, which gives no further energy to the illusion. Do not give the illusion to God, because this acknowledges something which does not exist. All that need be given to God is your willingness. The great thing about illusions is that they don't exist. When we invest no thing in them, they fall away, and only what is Real remains.

For a long time I saw differences between illusions. This thought was worse than another; this addiction was not as bad as something else. When you apply your belief system to illusions, you stay within the illusion. There are no differences within the illusion. One illusion is not bigger or more powerful than another. If we believe that an illusion has a great hold on us, we get caught up in the specifics of the illusion, like a dog chasing its tail. Similar to Truth, there are not various levels to illusion. This existence is really very simple. Either our eyes see all that truly exists, which is Truth, or our eyes see an appearance of something which does not exist.

Non-ordering of illusions means that you apply no judgment to them. Judgment is just another illusion. Without judgment, there is no differentiation. You initially recognize, without emotion or attachment, that illusion, as a whole, appears to exist. But once you recognize the illusion next to Truth, you know that illusion never existed. With Truth there are no questions, because there are no answers. Truth is self evident.

How can you know if you are in the illusion? One hallmark of illusion is seeing right and wrong and feeling like you are victimized because you were wronged. But we must neither run from nor counter an "attack" from another person. As with any illusion, we must see it for what it truly is, and that is a call for Love. Only then will it be transformed in our sight.

Can you "get out" of the illusion? You don't "get out" of the illusion by working in it. If you feel guilty over not being employed, taking a job to assuage the guilt leaves you in illusion, just in a different form. With illusion, we do not recognize that it doesn't exist, for this is a *recognition* of something that does not exist. We recognize what is Real, until the need for recognition falls away, as does everything else which is seen as if there were an observer. Nothing can be done to help the "process" along except to give your willingness to God. If you try to do something, like order or fight your thoughts, you only impede or "delay" your progress, within the illusion of time. Thought cannot be ordered or used to help you along. There are not some thoughts which are better or more consistent with the Reality of who you are, and "good" thoughts cannot be used to correct "bad" thoughts. All thought is illusion, for God is Stillness. Our brain or functioning mind in this existence is a tool for God to use, just as our feet are a tool for God to use when we need to walk, just as a car is a tool for God to use to help us quickly get from one point to another. Our mind is not an entity unto itself. It is not alive, not conscious of itself, although it believes this is true. We don't use the mind or direct the mind, because that is the mind directing the mind, still staying within the illusion. And the mind does not direct us. Can a hammer direct the building of a house? The mind is the means by which God can communicate to Itself while taking the appearance of being in a body.

It has been a long winter within the illusion. The Sun of Truth awakens all of us.

What does God think of the illusion? The entity we call God, the Stillness behind all, does not perceive. She only Loves. She does not "see" any of the illusions that you see about yourself. She sees only Herself, His Glory, His Love in you, as you. When you finally "see" this, then you simply Love, because you no longer see the illusions.

The belief in separation rests behind all illusions. What do you do with the illusion that you are separate and all of the far reaching roots that come off of that? Absolutely nothing.

☥

CHAPTER 23

Of Yourself

My journey has been one of becoming "of yourself." For a long time, I was fooled by my ego as I believed that I was spiritually superior. I wanted to know what this book could do for me instead of asking how I could help God achieve Her aims for the book, whether that meant one or one million copies sold. I had grandiose thoughts of being a famous author or a spiritual guru, and while I continued to entertain those thoughts, the book was going nowhere. As I shed my false beliefs in separation and specialness, I discovered that my true joy was found in my Oneness with God, which led to my realization that I could be doing anything and be joyous in that moment. This was especially true when I was of true service, when I became a clear reed, a container of Love through which God could act and show Her Love and forgiveness.

☥

"The meek shall inherit the earth." This statement, spoken by Jesus, goes further than just humility. It speaks of losing yourself in order to find your Self.

The extent to which God can use you is the extent to which you recognize that you are nothing of yourself. When you realize that you are small, like a little child, you know there is nothing for you to rely on but God. God provides *all* of your needs. It takes a while to realize that of yourself, you are nothing. Once you do, initially there is fear, because there is no turning back. There is no middle ground. The belief that you can rely only partially on God, and hence partially on yourself, is destroyed. What was reality before becomes very unstable ground. There is no choice but to surrender to the Truth of your Being, because God is the only Reality that exists.

For many years I believed that I was only the self which was represented in my personality. As part of this, I believed that this self gave me strength. When you see that this cannot be true, any return to this self for strength creates pain, fear, and despondency. God is your only source of strength. There is no relying on God *sometimes*. It is all or nothing. One way gives you complete peace, the other way, complete hell.

What is a good sign that you are no longer of yourself? When you become passionate about helping others (only if they choose to be helped) to remember God and His Love, you are no longer of yourself. Your joy flows from assisting them to discover their innate joy and passion without asking for or expecting anything in return from them. To Love, purely for the sake of Love.

Realizing that you are nothing of yourself is an evolution. Each day, each moment, you come to the knowing that God is the very Source of your Existence. Without Him, you would not have Being. To recognize this is to know obedience, not in the worldly sense, but in that you desire only to do His Will out of extreme Love and gratitude. Your concept, your understanding of your Being is totally changed. Of yourself, of the false image that you created and that you see, you are powerless. But as God created you, you are all powerful, you are all knowing, and you are Love, because these are the attributes of your Oneness. There is neither pride nor self adulation. There is only great humility and gratitude for what God has given to you. And there is neither self judgment nor judgment of others, because judgment does not exist. Only the infinite attributes of Love, peace, joy, and complete omniscience exist within you and everyone else. Time based reality is operated within but known to be false. Only the present moment exists, and in that moment God directs you as to His Will.

☥

CHAPTER 24

The Light

I first became aware of the nature of God through the variations in light. Since I started down this path, I have always loved to be in the woods, because the sunlight filtering through the trees reveals the beauty of the interplay of light and dark. This awareness of the variations in light helped me to see that I was also a part of that light, and hence I was an inseparable part of God. Just as the light filters in many different ways but is still the one light of the Sun, as the one ray of God we also appear in many different bodies and looks. I still think that these variations in light are one of the most beautiful things in the Universe. When I look at the stars or feel the warmth of the sun as it spreads over my body, I feel connected to all that is and I know that I am One with these heavenly bodies. We are made of the same essence. After all, God's creations are Light. Creation was birthed from a black hole. Astrophysicists now tell us that before the big bang there existed an entity infinitesimally smaller than anything they can measure today, and out of this came all that we know. Can you imagine? Can you remember?

☥

THE LIGHT

Is a beautiful sunset better than light filtering through the trees? Is a bright spotlight better than the moonlight? A spotlight may have the appearance of a higher magnitude, but it is not better. There is no better or worse. There is only the appearance of differences, allowing for contrast so that the infinite can know Itself. These variations of Light reveal God's true nature. Being in a body, having experiences, taking actions, thinking thoughts are all the appearance of variations in the light. No experience, no thought, no action, is better or worse than another.

Even in the darkness of the black hole there is light. Even within the appearance of the deepest evil, there is light. And if any light is present, it must be all light. How could there be partial light and partial darkness? The magnitude of the intensity of this light is infinite. There is one God. There is nothing brighter, nothing more powerful. There is nothing else. The appearance of darkness, the appearance of variations or shades of light, only serves as contrast to reveal the true and infinite nature of God.

How does the light reveal the nature of God, and how are we a part of that? Just as a prism reflects and refracts light, each of us reflects and refracts the Light of God. As a prism is moved, light will refract through it in new directions. Similarly, when each of us moves through life, interacting with the other facets of the prism, the appearance of constantly changing forms is created. We are the facet, and we are also the Light bouncing off and through each other in an infinite number of ways, creating unparalleled beauty. And that individualized Light that we are continues to bounce, to reflect and refract without end. Just as a ray of light within the prism extends itself and appears in many parts of the prism at the same time, each of us extends and appears in many realities simultaneously.

How do we see anything? We see something by the reflection of light from it. God sees Himself, is aware of Herself, through reflection. In addition to prisms, all forms of Creation act as mirrors, and the reflection gives the appearance of light and dark. It gives contrast. What is the dark? It is an appearance of an absence of the *Light*. Each of us is also a reflection of God, created through this dance of light and dark. The paradox you must stay present in is reconciling the appearance of light and dark within the world, and especially within yourself, while knowing that you are only Light. We exist both as the Son and as the One.

Open your eyes. Look around. You are seeing a reflection of yourself. The Light is within you and pours forth from you.

CHAPTER 25

Sin and Sacrifice

The belief in sin originated with the concept that you can somehow separate yourself from God. This thought system was a central part of my experience that somehow I had offended and wronged God by leaving Him, and in doing so I sinned, producing tremendous guilt within me. Taking that a step further, I lived with a fear that I would be punished for sinning. Now I see how incompatible these beliefs I held were with a God I know to be Love. God loves. He does not withhold and punish, but many in our society try to equate their human experience of a parent with the Divine. A human parent loves conditionally, often using a carrot and stick approach. God just loves. That is all She can do, for that is all She is. Even in the last few years I have tended to forget and equate my mistakes with sin. For example, my wife and I have headstrong teenagers, and although I have gotten much better, I will still yell at my son. This is something I want to completely change. If I beat myself up about it, if I judge myself for doing it, I am seeing it as a sin, because I am reverting to a belief system of good and bad as we discussed early in the book. But if I see it as a mistake that I want to correct the next time, then I am simply residing in the paradox. The paradox is that there is no sin and everything is perfect as it is, yet I want to correct my mistake and change the behavior.

It is ironic that we have used the very thing which has given us Life and our existence and turned it so that it is what blinds us to our divinity and prevents us from feeling immense Love and joy. The appearance of separation is simply a way for God to have an experience of Itself, and we are the expression of that experience. Yet, because we believe that the appearance is reality, we judge the separation and see it as sinful, cutting us off from Love, joy and peace. God is still having the experience of Itself, and this experience is only Love, but within this play we call Life here on Earth, it does not appear as Love.

Our society is one where everyone moves from "pleasure" to "pleasure," always looking for happiness, always being disappointed because true joy can only be found in God. We want the perfect job, the bigger house, the peak sexual experience. We look for our soulmate, the one with whom can spend the rest of our life in loving bliss. We look, and when we do not find, or it appears that we find and then it does not bring us happiness, we numb the pain of an impossible search through drugs or alcohol, workaholism, sugar, television or computer, exercise, or any number of creative ways man has devised. We believe this world is real, thus we have created a belief in sacrifice, a belief that we can either lose something of value, or it can be taken from us. This belief is what prevents us from seeing what we are truly searching for, which is our "return" to union with God in Love. Jesus was crucified for the belief in sacrifice. He was the symbol for our belief in sin, and those who crucified him believed that if they could project their sins on to him, then they would be free of sin. Their belief was, and is the world's belief today, that the body was the symbol and the repository of sin, and with Jesus' death and the destruction of his body, the sins that they had projected on to him would be destroyed also. Once they destroyed this representation of God, they had triumphed over Him, and they had preempted His vengeful wrath against them over their sins. Since they had "won" and they had eliminated their sins against Him, maybe this bloodthirsty and vengeful God would take pity on them and no longer withhold or take away pleasures of the world. As long as our belief in sacrifice remains, we cannot see God as Love. So we move from one pleasure to the next, like a dog chasing its tail, never going to the root of the belief. Sacrifice is an illusion. Nothing in this world can be given or taken, because nothing in this world is real. All that is Real, all that the Father has, all that the Mother has, is already yours. It was not given to you, because you have always had it.

This illusion of sacrifice originates from the belief that we are separate and that something can be better than another, the belief that differences exist. Not only does a belief in sacrifice apply to the pleasures of the world, but it also applies to the "negative" aspects, such as anger, self judgment, fear, and guilt. We use these illusory mechanisms to create a belief that one can control a situation. We do not want to sacrifice our victimhood. Giving up the belief in sacrifice does not mean that you do not indulge in the pleasures of the world, nor does it mean that you do not show emotion. What it means is that you know these things will not give you a certain outcome. A pleasure of the world will not make you happy. Getting angry or acting like a victim will not control a situation. No one is a victim, and control does not exist. Can a drop of water control the flow and direction of the river?

What does the crucifixion represent? It represents the death, the crossing out of the belief that we can be separate. Sacrifice is not possible, and sin does not exist, because there has never been and there can never be a change to the One. We are as we were created in the one holy moment. We can never cause God to withhold his Love, because we are One with God and that Love. Jesus allowed himself to be put to death so that Truth would be revealed. By allowing the illusion of sacrifice to be carried out to such an extreme degree, he created a huge contrast to Truth, and in doing so he also opened the door for the illusion of sin to be dissolved in that light of Truth, for sacrifice and sin stand together. In the illusory eyes of the world, his sacrificial death should have absolved everyone of all sin and brought about a heaven on Earth. Yet, today the world still sees sin, and both individually and collectively the belief in the necessity of sacrifice is carried forward, where it is projected as blame toward individuals, groups, or nations.

Sin can be described as an error which can be corrected through the proper vision of an awakened mind. What are some of the most common sins? One is seeing with a limited perspective and believing that this limited perspective is Truth. Even if in the slightest way, you feel the need to defend, to yourself or another person, a thought or statement, you are not seeing with eyes of wholeness. Along this same line is not being truthful with yourself about yourself. We push our beliefs about ourselves into the deepest corners of our psyche, because we fear those beliefs and we fear what God will do if He "sees" the "truth." Nothing can be hidden from yourself or from God. I am as I am. It is as it is. When you see the foolishness of trying to hide something, you no longer fear it.

Why is sinlessness all there is? If this were not the case, the universe would be chaos. What would determine the line between sin and sinlessness? And who would make that determination---God? Based on what value system? Would the smallest "negative" thought make you full of sin? Every situation, every circumstance, is different. (Notice the similarities to the arbitrariness of appearances and of your belief system?) If some circumstances were sinful, and some were not, that would be total chaos. And since God is everything, God would be total chaos. God cannot be arbitrary, or we would exist in total chaos. Either everything is sinless, or everything is full of sin, and the latter would mean we exist and have our being in total chaos.

☥

CHAPTER 26

The Mind

As I stated earlier in the book, my mind has been very active all of my life. It has been an excellent organizing tool, but at the same time it has been a large impediment to my progress on this path. Or has it? The Mind of God and your localized mind, or ego, exemplify the paradox that provides the balanced tension of Life. In this bodily form, one cannot exist without the other. The paradox always helps you to see Life from all angles. When I began this journey, all I knew was the localized mind. I could never have envisioned that there was something else, that this was not all there was. I mentioned earlier in the book about the first time my soul, my spirit, my God self revealed itself when I was sitting in my car. Actually, it is not true to say that it revealed itself. This was the first time I became aware of it, and even this statement is accurate only for how I viewed it at that time. As the years passed, I had greater awareness of the thoughts I shared with God, but it would be very disconcerting when I could not "hold" this space. I was continuing to see a difference between the two minds, and at that point my localized mind seemed like the enemy as it generated many and frequent thoughts of judgment. But in retrospect, these disconcerting thoughts acted as a well defined contrast to my true thoughts, and this helped me to be aware of my true thoughts. In turn, this evolved to where I was able to "hold" this true space the vast majority of time.

THE MIND

What is this "split" or "localized mind?" Most of us live in an illusion that we are a consciousness or a mind that exists as its own center, an entity unto itself which sees God, everyone, and everything as separate. Because it has no basis in reality, this split mind is constantly looking for affirmations of its existence, without success. Your split mind is the source of your fears, of your desires, of your need to be something other than you are, of your need to be special. It is the reason you get angry, the reason you want to have more or be better than the next person. It is the source of your suffering. This is one view from the paradox.

At some point on your journey, you come to the realization that there is more than this mind which you have identified with. You see that you have lived and operated in this world with the appearance of a split mind and that this split mind has always feared itself, seeing itself as localized to a body and separate from everything. When you operate from this split mind, it feels as if you are standing on constantly shifting ground, because you see with false vision. You cling to your beliefs and to some type of identity in an unsuccessful attempt to feel safe. Yet this realization of a split mind is also the opening that allows God and divine Love to reenter into your remembrance. Knowing that it was not God that you feared but yourself, you call for God to help you correct this belief in a split. And you are grateful, as you realize that the very thing which seems like an obstacle, the very thing which is split, is also the gift which enables God to come into your recognition and remembrance.

This split mind does not steer the boat, although it believes it does. The River of Life carries you along, and the mind is like a hair on your head that is along for the ride.

Imagine that you feel a slight sensation of a small bug crawling on you. Now, imagine that you are the bug, and your mind and thoughts are running rampant. Something like: "How did I get here? I am so scared, because I don't know where I am at. I am not worth anything because I can't do anything right. Maybe I should sting this leg to protect myself. It's kill or be killed. This is a cruel world. I've let everyone down." Now, no longer are you the bug. You still feel only the slightest of sensations, and you have no sense of the lunacy that is passing through the bug's mind.

You will know with certainty the very first time your perspective is "outside" the localized mind, the first time your thoughts originate from the Mind of God, from Love, because the contrast will be so great. Until this occurrence, it is the mind fooling the mind. When your perspective is outside the mind, you are spontaneously joyful, filled with laughter and a strong desire to express God's Love. You feel completely safe as part of Creation. Fear does not exist.

If the mind is still confirming the reality of Allness, then the dog is still chasing its tail. Allness needs no confirmation, no recognition. Allness includes the mind, not the other way around. With Allness, you are the awareness behind the aware.

Are you still confused? Are you the judgment, the observer of the judgment, or nothingness?

As Oneness, Spirit observes the mind and its gyrating, just as it observes other parts of Itself. It does not judge the workings of the mind, for it is not capable of judgment. It sees only Itself appearing in a form. Spirit may observe the stark terror that the mind feels when it realizes that it is not the center of the world, but there is no emotion attached to this observation. If your perspective reverts back to one that the mind sees, then this terror is felt as fear, a physically based emotion. From the view of wholeness, as Spirit you know that the mind is not your enemy. It is a beautiful gift, a tool to be used to enhance the experience of being in a body. As an expression of God, your experience can be one where throughout your whole life your view never steps outside the mind, or it can be one where it does. It does not matter. Every experience is joyful and holy.

What should be done with a very active mind? Let everything be as it is. This includes the mind. When you no longer try to control the mind, when you no longer act as its jailer, the mind is like a caged animal which has been set free and which takes full advantage of its freedom to roam and create havoc. The mind generates thoughts which go in an endless number of directions and scenarios. But since you are no longer the jailer, you can let the mind do what it wants. You are not responsible for it, and you do not have to be aware of what it is saying or doing. Eventually, your awareness of it becomes very small, like a small itch or a gentle breeze. When you need it, like you need a hammer to hit a nail, you simply use it.

Examine your beliefs around your mind. Do you have a belief that your mind is powerful and cannot be controlled, that it is more than just another part of the body, more than just a tool to be used by God? Or do you have a belief that you can control your unruly mind? Either way, you are assigning an importance to the mind which does not exist. Your belief is giving energy to an illusion, creating an appearance that does not exist. It is this illusion which is desirous of finding God, of finding love, and it creates the search. Yet, that which you already are cannot be searching for something that it is. Allness does not need to search for Itself. Do you see that this illusory mind is where your fear, your guilt, your self judgment is generated from? You come to a place where you can no longer live a lie, where you can no longer live as something you are not.

Within the paradox, all angles are represented. Even a split mind is not separate from the One, from Love. The only purpose for the appearance of cracks in the egg is to see that the egg was never cracked and has always been whole. The mind Loves to such an extreme degree. It takes on the appearance of guilt, shame, fear, self judgment, hatred, to show you that you are Love. It reflects the contrast and paradox of the whole, as it wants "something" to happen while at the same time it is fearful of something happening. The instability of the mind reflecting the paradox is what spurs your remembrance.

When the only desire is to Love Her, no matter the consequences, no matter the result, even if it means death, the balance of the scale has tipped. As does every part of the One, the mind desires wholeness. Having been released from the cage and no longer desiring to be on the outside creating trouble, it also surrenders to God. It turns in its orientation so that The Mind of God can flow through it freely, and it becomes the tool that it was meant to be. Instead of being an obstruction, it now serves as an amplifier, boosting the communication link between the heart of the Father and His Son.

☥

CHAPTER 27

The Witness

I started to change my behaviors and how I looked at myself when I first began witnessing my actions and then my thoughts. The witnessing showed me that change was possible. It seemed to me that I was of two minds while I was witnessing. When I would rage, the witnessing would bring the level of intensity down greatly. Sometimes I would completely stop in the middle of the raging and walk away. A number of times I would simply smile in realization of how childish I was acting and how silly it was to get mad over anything. Always, the peace of that witnessing mind flowed throughout my body. Although this might not be considered the same witnessing as above, occasionally I would stare at myself in a mirror. As my eyes looked at my eyes, I would see the depths within myself and I would remember that I was not this body that I temporarily inhabit.

☥

If you want to spur your remembrance, witness everything that goes on with you. Right now, witness your belief about witnessing. My experience was one where I witnessed every moment, especially my thoughts. Sometimes my thoughts were not in accordance with what I would have liked, but the thought content was irrelevant. What was important was that I was witnessing the thought, and I was witnessing that I didn't like the thought. See how it works?

If consciously you create a form that you want to change such as an emotion or an experience, simply recognize it is only the appearance of energy in form. It is only an expression of God, similar to God in costume, not God Itself. Withdrawing your consciousness toward that form eliminates the appearance of the form, allowing God to be Itself.

In the early stages it is enough to witness, without judgment, when you have a reaction. You don't even need to know what the reaction is about. As you progress, you can witness your emotions, your thoughts, but most of all, witness your self, your identity as a complete and separate entity. When you have observed enough times, your remembrance becomes concrete, and the concept of you, or you as a separate self, becomes meaningless.

When you cling to the belief that you have an identity, you form your own special world, your own unique prison cell, and your eyes see what is required to validate that identity. When you drop the concept of an observer and the concept that you have an identity, you rest in the stillness, in the One.

When you cease to observe the One, you know no separation as the One. However, observation of the undifferentiated energy, of the One, is a necessary prerequisite to know that only the One exists. The contrast reveals God.

CHAPTER 28

Duality

As I walk through the world awake, I walk as the Son or as the One, the Father being all that exists. This alternation is like a see saw that is always in movement. Without the Son, the Father could not be known as the Father. Without the Father, the Son would not be recognized as the Son. This balance has defined Duality for me.

Duality is the counterpoint to Oneness, the black to the white. In order to know Oneness, you must know Duality. One does not exist without the recognition of the other.

Seeing "good" and "bad" does not separate you from God. If you believe you are separate, then your vision sees good and bad. Seeing good and bad then acts as false reinforcement, or proof, that your belief in separation is true. What we see "outside" our Self is only a projection of what we see "inside" our Self, for outside and inside are not separate. If we see separation or differences in the world, it flows from our belief in duality, our belief that we are separate from God.

What is it that you push away most? That is Oneness calling you, showing you. What is it that you are most attracted to? Is it the Oneness? That is the Oneness calling you, showing you. Every direction you turn, every thought you have, even the belief in Duality, is the Oneness. The paradox is resolved in the One.

If you still distinguish periods in your life between non-connected/fear states and connected/oneness states, you are reinforcing and perpetuating a duality which does not exist. You believe in appearances. Duality is the vehicle in which you can see the Oneness revealed in everything, both as the experience of Oneness (the connected state), and as the *contrast* to the experience of Oneness (the non-connected state).

We cannot recognize something as Love if we are recognizing it as separate. The appearance of Duality is reinforced by the recognition of Duality. What if we could see the Oneness that is present in the Duality, the appearance of differences? Rejoice in the appearance of differences, for this is the richness of Life, the way for you as the Divine to know Itself in an infinite number of ways.

☥

CHAPTER 29

Creation

*After I finished the first version of this book, I was amazed by it, and I felt blessed to have been given the opportunity to have been a part of God's Love in such a way. I also felt immense Love coming from the book to me, because this is what our Creations do. As I created from Love, I was blessed many times over by Love coming back from my Creation. My Father, your Father, our Mother, created her Son in Love. As part of the Sonship, when I created this book, I extended His Love, and I also knew what it was truly like to be a Co-Creator. There are no differences between Creations that are birthed in Love. This book is not more important than the garden you created or the project you did at work. The beauty and divinity lie in my **act** of Creation, not in the book itself.*

☥

If Love is the engine of the universe, then Creation is the fuel. The two work hand in hand. This book, this creation, was created from Love. It is God's Love to me, His Love to

Himself, His Love to you, and my Love to you. And they are all the same.

The fox, the hawk, the oak tree, every living thing, has in its DNA, has as its very Being, the drive to recreate itself. Creation is the essence of God. This essence is expressed through Love. God, as Love, creates through Love. All of us as the Sonship, created by Love, also create through Love.

We can create any form, "positive" or "negative," but it is still Love. For instance, self judgment is a form. We create self judgment just as we create joy, our physical bodies, or our experiences. The important word is create. God knows Itself through Creation. God is Love, and Creation is the expression of that Love, bringing great joy that God's very essence and the purpose of existence is being fulfilled. As One with God, we create from Love. Although forms *appear* different, Love is the energy that is every form, thus no form is "better" or "worse" than another. The joy is in the creation, not in the form that is created. As we have forgotten the Truth of our Being and our Oneness, we have lumped creation upon creation. Self judgment is only undifferentiated energy appearing in form, but we have a belief (a second creation) that it is bad. We do that with many forms, and it becomes difficult to wade through these creative forms, these illusions, which are intertwined and lumped upon each other. We feel separate from God when we judge our creations as bad.

If you want to change something, you need only to withdraw your consciousness from it, allowing you to see the energy as its true state. Your consciousness can be directed in many ways to manifest or create a certain form or appearance of the energy. The energy can be formed on the mental, spiritual, physical, or emotional planes, like a thought, a belief, a desire, or a physical condition. Because only the present moment exists, you can change anything from the past, and it can be changed in an infinite number of ways, depending on the consciousness you give to it. When you no longer give a past event any consciousness, it ceases to appear in the form you knew it and in any form at all. It returns to its undifferentiated state in the great primordial energy soup pot.

This primordial energy of the One can take on the appearance of anything. We are co-creators, and we use the energy to form thought, emotion, and experiences. We are each using the energy to take on the appearance of a physical body. The energy can be used consciously, as Jesus did, or it can be used unconsciously, as is the case for the vast majority. When we use it consciously, we are able to hold the paradox. We know that we are the One while we hold the appearance of being separate, or the One in many forms. In this conscious state we create from Love, which brings us great joy.

Creation. Creativity. Our creativity is inseparable from our inheritance as co-creators with God. As we increasingly recognize our Oneness, our creativity blossoms. We express what we are---Love. There is a great joy and love in what we do, and this is manifested in the final result, whether that is poetry, building a house, painting, playing chess, fixing cars, parenting, or anything. Ministering, simply expressing love and kindness is an act of creativity, an act of Creation, which encompasses all of the rest. Creation creates Itself. The engine of the universe is the expression of Love. When Love is expressed, whether it appears to be received or not, it is magnified a thousandfold. Creation is expansive. When we express Love, God expands, further awakening to Himself.

God creates through extension of Herself. She is complete in her Creation. Each of us is completed in our Creation, and our Creations are completed in their Creations, creating an infinite succession, all originating back to the Source, the One. A small trickle of Love high in the mountains becomes a stream, which then becomes the source for numerous rivers of Love, all joyously cascading down, level after level, to eventually fill and nourish the very lowest areas, oceans of Love. Our Creations have always been completed, but within the illusion of time, they await our return and their completion. As we complete our Creations, we are completed through extension, just as God is completed through us.

As we Love our Creations, we can remember the infinite Love that God has for us, his Creation. And as we move deeper into our Love for our Creations, this propels us deeper, joyously surrendering into our Love for God. Just as we are an extension of God's Love, our Creations extend our Love, and thus His Love by extension. Everything we create, whether it is a project at work, a letter, a book, or a family meal, is of God and has a consciousness of Love running through it. No Creation is better than another. Each is holy. As these Creations go forth into the world, they extend our Love, God's Love, to everything they contact.

We live in the Truth of our Being, that we are the One taking the appearance of parts, when we acknowledge and surrender ourselves as an extension of the Creator, a clear vessel through which God can Create and Love his Creations.

☥

CHAPTER 30

Love

When I was around twelve to thirteen, I was sexually abused by my mother. This had huge ramifications for how I saw myself, how I saw the world, and eventually how I saw my relationship with God. Since it happened during puberty, my concept of love was greatly distorted. How could someone who supposedly loved me do this to me? How did love and sexuality fit together? I felt tremendous shame and guilt that somehow I had caused this to happen. As I went through therapy, the anger and rage at my mother poured out of me many, many times. I also experienced a large amount of sadness and grief at having my innocence and my childhood taken from me, as well as not having a "normal mother."

My mother had been abused herself as a child, and in a small way, this helped me to understand the "why" behind the act. But it also gave me the resolution to break the pattern and end the legacy with me. Why do I tell you this? For many reasons. First, I hope that it provides comfort for you in knowing that it is possible to heal from sexual abuse or other emotional traumas you have gone through. You do not have to live with the anger or the guilt the rest of your life. No, you can't go back and change the act, but you can see it in a different light. As I worked through my concept of distorted love *that had come about as a result of the abuse, I was also working on a new understanding of God's Love for me. For I saw God as separate from me. I saw Him as an unforgiving parent who would punish you when you sin, not the parent who created His Son from Himself and who Loves His Son unconditionally in a magnitude incomprehensible to the human mind. As part of what I wanted to work on in this dream called life, I chose the experience of abuse so that it would bring up the unresolved issues I had around God's Love. My mother, as an expression of God, helped me to fulfill what I wanted to work on and achieve in this lifetime. As a personality or ego, she was asleep, but at the real level of her Being, her act was an immense gesture of Love. As the one Son (the Sonship), we all work together in this dream to awaken us to remembrance of God's true nature and His Love. Let me be clear that this higher perspective came gradually and I spiraled in and out of it. You cannot skip to this perspective and be free of your limiting and illusory beliefs without first examining and clearing these beliefs. These beliefs come from emotional blockages where you are frozen in time from an earlier period, like your childhood. If you have suffered a serious trauma like abuse, you <u>must</u> work on and release this anger, grief, shame, and guilt when they arise in you. This will probably entail a great deal of fear in looking at these past issues, and it may involve a lot of hard work. As I re-experienced these issues, in the early years I called it suffering, but I came to see these issues as gifts, because they brought me back to myself, to God. If you do not clear these blockages and limiting beliefs, you cannot move to the higher perspective, which entails stripping away all that is false so that only the divine remains. Your ego can tell you that you don't have to look at these issues and that you are past all of that because it is not real, but you are fooling yourself. As long* as you hold those limiting beliefs, you **make** it real for you. If you are truly honest with yourself, you will know when you have seen through the false underpinnings of these beliefs, enabling you to make a leap in your consciousness and perspective.

The abuse is my "secret" that I have told you. You may have a secret of your own that you are trying to keep, because you believe that you would die if someone found out, but please realize that there are no secrets. God is everywhere, all knowing. You are One with everything, and your secret belongs to everyone. You may have experienced it in your body, but bodies are illusory and are only seen through eyes of separation, not eyes of Oneness. As I no longer identified with my body as all that I am, I no longer felt any guilt or shame around what happened, and this is what awaits you as well. What happened to you, happened to God and was done by God!

Love is *the* essence of all that is. It is the trunk from which all roots and branches spring forth, spanning heaven and Earth. Rejoice, for this is a place of incredible joy and peace. This place is you. We are here to be the embodiment of this Love. It is that simple. Always remember and return to that. Even in the appearance of the deepest darkness, the Sun of your heart shines beyond all brilliance.

Love has been my path since the beginning, and for that I am grateful. At times the longing has been very painful, and I have suffered as all that is not pure and divine is burned in the fire of His Love, but I would not change anything. Each of us, as Love, must eventually return on the path of Love. The return of the Son to the Father-Mother.

What is this Divine Love and how is it different from human love? Human love is conditional. It has strings attached, expectations and hidden requirements that are placed on another. Human love is an appearance like everything else in the world. Divine Love has no conditions. It Loves regardless of whether the appearance of Love is returned to it. A mother's love for her children is the closest representation to Divine Love, but even this love is but a faint image of the Love shared between you and God. Jesus recognized his Oneness and became that divine Love, loving even those who crucified him, for he saw only God, he saw only himself in them. Divine Love is infinite in magnitude, always there, awaiting your "return." Like the water tossing itself over the rocks of the waterfall with abandon and without regard to Itself, Love gives of Itself, wholly and unceasingly. And when you know yourself as this Love, everything is seen and recognized as Love, beauty, and gentleness.

Divine Love embodies the call of God to His Beloved. The call is always there, whether we hear it or not. Each of us has an immense longing to return to our Source, to return to that Love. When we live in the illusion and duality of a physical body, it appears that we are as far from that Source as could be. Yet, this "distance" only heightens the contrast, magnifying the longing until it is so painful that we propel ourselves back to our home. In the end, this call of Love is all that matters. It is all there is.

There is nothing you can do, nothing you can say, nothing you can think which would cause God to cease loving you, for you are One with that Love. All that exists, all that has meaning, is the direct Love relationship with God. That is where the eternal peace and unlimited joy lie. When you are present in this Love, you are so overcome with gratitude that it can bring you to tears in any moment. Why did Jesus wash the feet of his disciples? Because he was washing the feet of God. When you live and breathe from that state of being, everything else becomes irrelevant, with appearances fading into the background. Love is why we are here. That is the only way we are fulfilled. We still operate in the world, but we remain fully grounded and existing in that Love, and we love Him and all of His Creation as ourselves. That does not mean that we do not enjoy being in the world; for this is one of an infinite number of playgrounds where the consummation of your relationship with God can be revealed and expressed.

When Jesus said no one comes to the Father except through me, he was saying that you come only through Love, for as The Christ, as Love, he returned in his consciousness to Oneness with God. Through Love, each of us takes the same journey, remembering our Oneness, remembering that we have never left our Source.

While we are Love, we are also experiencing Love. We *appear* to have a consciousness separate from God, so that God as Love, can experience Itself. The body of God, the body of Love, is like clay. Through the appearance of having an experience, it can be formed into any number of shapes and designs. But in the end, it is still Love.

The alternation of valleys and mountaintops, of our consciousness between connected and non-connected states, is the manna by which Love can be experienced. These create form, a way for God to know Himself. Without the valley, there could be no mountaintop. When we feel the absence of Love, it is our longing to return to Love which defines Love and creates an infinite expression of it. The form or state is irrelevant.

Love is experienced every day in close relationships, and often we miss the call for Love, which is still Love. If you are in a close relationship where friction exists, it is like two diamonds polishing each other. That friction, that frustration you feel, is the greatest gift of Love that you are both giving as well as receiving, for if you stay present in the friction and don't run, the friction will show you who you really are. The greater the falsity, the greater is the contrast to the Love that you are, and the more that God, as Love, is revealed in your partner.

In addition to your relationships, the Love you feel for anything is the Love you feel for God. It is one and the same. Everything you encounter in Life, *everything and everyone*, has the sole purpose of bringing about a remembrance of the deep Love affair and relationship you have with your Creator. That is why we exist, taking the appearance of being separate. Consciousness becomes the Creator and is fulfilled only through Love. God wants only to pour Her infinite Love on you, and nothing else. With unlimited patience, She will wait an "eternity" until you remember, and all of heaven will cry tears of joy when you do.

Like the flower which unfolds its petals to the light of the sun, becoming that which it is and can only be, our heart unfolds to the Love of God, expressing our true nature. And for both us and the flower, the angels sing with joy at the fulfillment of Creation.

If we are against anything, we are against Love, for it is all Love. Our beliefs cover the face of Christ, the face of Love. We cling to those beliefs, because we believe that keeps us safe, yet it is exactly the opposite.

Compassion is Love in action. True compassion does not come from a place of pity. It arises from deep within and flows from Love. It sees but does not judge. It is very gentle.

How do you operate in the world with this Love? Seeing only Love and knowing yourself to be that Love does not mean that you do not operate and take care of what is needed to do in the world. You are Love, but your appearance in form is in a world that has the appearance of differences. You take out the garbage, and you discipline the kids. You ask to speak to a supervisor when you are not getting a satisfactory response, and you withhold payment from a contractor who has not performed work properly. All of these are still Love. Love does not have a certain look. It appears as all forms---kindness, joy, anger, cancer, peace, natural disaster, war. Regardless of the form or appearance, it is still Love.

There are several points along this journey of Love that can be recognized, some reappearing numerous times within the spiral. One such place is a strong desire to do God's Will, to Love wholly and completely without regard or belief in a separate self. This is Creation. The more Love that is given, the more Love that is received. This becomes our only purpose in this life on Earth, and this is what brings joy and peace. As we move into this state of being, we know our Oneness with the Father, and at the same time we retain an appearance of Self, for this is required to consummate and express joyously in each moment our relationship with the Beloved. This is how Love knows Itself. Our acts of Love, our acts of Creation, are expressed simultaneously from the Father and for the Father.

Another place along the journey is the Longing, a place that feels very painful, a place where it feels almost impossible to continue living as we are. Everything becomes meaningless except our Love for Him, and that which we want so badly, Union, cannot occur through our force of Will. Everyone walking this Earth feels this deep longing to be filled by God, but few recognize it and very few shed their beliefs to uncover this Love. Most attempt to medicate the tremendous pain of this longing with addictions: drugs or alcohol, food, sugar, television or computer, sex, work, anger, exercise, emotional dramas, living only in the future---the list is endless. If you are brave enough to see through your beliefs and stay present in the longing, it is very painful, but it is also joyous, because your Love for Him completely opens your heart. This is the time when the veil is so thin, but you cannot lift it. If you cannot stay present and you pull back from the pain, you look again to the world and its trinkets to fill the longing. During these interim periods, it feels as if you are the walking dead. You are not being who you really are. Love can never be covered, and it calls you back, bringing you into that deep remembrance and need for Union, and starting the whole cycle again. The cycle stops when the pain of not feeling the Love is greater than the pain of not having your Love fulfilled.

The Longing, the pain, that *is* what is. When we stay in it and of it, when we no longer run from it, we accept our true being and we surrender. The Longing is the tree trunk into which all roots, all paths, merge. It is the state that came about the moment you were created, the one holy moment you rest in.

As you look around you, you see that She is everywhere, in everything and everyone. This is all for you, all for you to remember how much She loves you. It is as if nothing exists but you and Her, and this *is* the way it is. It is beyond comprehension, beyond understanding. You see and meet Her every moment, as She calls to you, "see me here, see me here. See the extent I would go to show you my Love."

Author's note

Are you having a problem with this book and all of the paradoxical, conflicting statements? Do you want answers in your life and you don't feel like you are getting them, or are you understanding something and then later it makes no sense? I understand; I've been there many times, including periods when I was working on this book. Or do you think that this book and its message is a bunch of bunk? Did it make you raging mad, because if so, I am amazed that you made it to the end. That is a testament to your perseverance and your desire to know Truth. If you think the book has no worth, then thank you for that blessing. For without you and others who dislike the book providing the contrast, this book would not become "real" for those who are attracted to the message. It takes two to tango. It is extremely natural and understandable to say that God is this or that this is the way reality is based on what *your* vision has seen up until this point. That is exactly where you are supposed to be. And for those who argued the world was flat, that was where they were meant to be, and in one sense, the world was flat, because that was where they were at the time. If you can give yourself

AUTHOR'S NOTE

one gift, allow God to show you and take you *wherever* you are meant to be. Nothing can be shown or revealed to you that is bad, because God is One. Maybe we will find out that the world is square. I don't dismiss any possibility. It is a lot more fun that way. Whether this message resonates with you or not is not the issue. You are living life and I am living life, and what an adventure it is. Enjoy!

Further Steps Along The Journey

Are you happy?

Joy is your birthright. If you are not happy, do you want to "change" your situation? If so, do you believe that you can achieve that by changing something outside of you---your job, your possessions, your relationships? All that needs to be changed is your vision, how you view your situation. When you change that, you change the world. See the world as it is, not as you see it.

What is Enlightenment?

Enlightenment, cosmic consciousness, nirvana are all words in a language. They are unsuccessful attempts by grabbing and searching minds to apply a finite meaning to something which is infinite. If we see a patch of green water in the blue ocean, would we say that the patch was better than the rest of the ocean or that it was no longer the ocean? Just as the patch of green water seamlessly integrates with the surrounding ocean, there is only the appearance of differentiation with events that life brings to us. There can be no change to the One.

Enlightenment is the passing away of all illusions, including the belief in a split mind. But none of these illusions existed in the first place. Enlightenment is "in the Light." We only need to recognize that we are already wholly of the Light. It is much like walking into a darkened room and turning on the light. We know things are present in the room. We just don't see exactly what is there until we flip the switch and illuminate everything. Of course, this illumination can happen in an instant, because an instant is all that exists. And you have always been in that room.

What does being present mean?

Have you ever been, not just felt, but *been* the sensation of your foot as it is placed on the ground for each step? Just slow down, and be aware of every muscle preparing to do its job. What about the sensation of your hair touching your skin? Or the sensation of the wind blowing across your face? Do you judge the wind and say it is cold, or are you simply aware that something is interacting with your face, without assigning good or bad? When we are present in our body, we are present in the infinite body of God. There is no separation. And when we are present in the infinite body, we are present in the now. They are one and the same.

What is the peace of God?

The peace of God is your natural state. It is a peace that is always present, a peace that is inherent in your Oneness with

God and his Will. It is not a peace as the world sees it, which is the *appearance* of a cessation of fear derived from the covering of fear. If you are fearful about money, only an illusory peace results from taking a higher paying job. The fear is still there. The peace of God flows from you when you recognize that fear was never there.

Are we God, or are we a part of God?

Both. Neither. When you look at a wave breaking on the beach, you say that it is the ocean. But is it the complete ocean, the whole body of water? When you see a difference by distinguishing between the wave and the surrounding ocean, does that mean the wave is separate? What happens to a particular wave when it releases its form back into the ocean? If there were absolutely no waves and the water were perfectly still, what does it become? It is still the ocean.

When the feeling of Longing is present, why is it important to stay in it?

The Longing to be fulfilled by God and His Love is our natural state. It is the emptiness, the appearance of the absence of Love, the round hole in which the peg of manifestation fits perfectly. You are the Longing, and everything in, through, and around you is Love. As the clear vessel of Longing, you provide the container which holds and defines the Love, allowing the Love to pass in and around and through the container. The container also provides the form which prevents the deep pain of the Longing, which is so intense that it brings you to tears, from spilling out as anger at those around you. Without our being the container of Longing, God could not know His Love. Ironically, we have believed that we are guilty for separating from God and that we are guilty for not being able to heal that separation through a consummation of Love. Yet, the paradox that exists is that we know God's Love through not being fulfilled by that Love. The Longing is one side of the balanced scale, one side of the paradox. When we feel the Longing, it is as if God is outside of us. We are the Son. When the Longing is not present, you feel complete, the One, the other side of the scale. This dance between the two is the paradox, the interplay of being the whole continuum with the appearance of being a set point on it.

What does it mean to be a container?

Each of us acts as a container to give form to the formless. Since Love is all that Is, each container holds Love, giving form and existence to that Love. Just as Love takes on different appearances, it appears that as a container we hold these various appearances: joy, grief, anger, guilt, fear, self judgment, etc. When "negative" appearances such as fear or guilt arise, we often attempt to project these away in order not to feel them. But when they arise, if we create a container for them, we are accepting them as they are. This acceptance leads to dissolution of their appearance. As you create a container of yourself, as you become a clear vessel, you acknowledge your Oneness, your Love.

What is the fear of God?

The fear of God is fear of yourself, for you are One with Him. It is the fear of Love, the fear of allowing Her Love to completely engulf you. The fear of God also arises from the belief that you can have a will that is separate from the Will of God. That belief leads to guilt and your fear that you have usurped His power. And if you are in opposition to God, He will punish you. Thus, it is a kill or be killed scenario. As is the case with all illusions, when we give no energy to them and we recognize Truth, they dissipate into the unreality from which they were born.

When we don't feel God's presence what is happening?

We feel separate because of our beliefs and judgments about our actions, our thoughts, or even about our beliefs. But feeling separate is only an experience which will pass like all experiences. Nothing can make us separate. Oneness is eternal. One of the most entrenched illusions is the belief that if we think thoughts or take actions which "sin" against God, creating a feeling that we are separate, then we truly are separate, and, that we have done something to create this separation. But the effect cannot create the cause. The feeling of separation cannot create separation. Separation from God is not possible. When this belief is carried to its extreme, it results in rage and blame, which is an unsuccessful attempt by someone to project their self judgment on to individuals, on to the world, on to their circumstances, and on to God. They self judge because they believe that they have created the separation or that they should be doing something to bring themselves back to God. If the anger is not allowed expression, it turns inward and results in depression, and the blame turns inside out, as they assume the role of victim. The greatest gift you can give yourself is to remember that even when the clouds of illusion seem to blot out the Sun, God walks with you always, that He is closer than your breath. Is not your feeling of separation and your belief in it Him also? Allow the Sun to shed its Light on your beliefs, dissipating the fog immediately.

What are you willing to do to know God and His Love?

Are you willing to walk through hell to get there? For you are Heaven, but you believe that you live in hell. You may have seen only a little bit of the scenery, because you have stayed fairly stationary. Maybe it is time to take a road trip to see how far hell goes. Like a house that has been condemned, hell is just another illusion that will pass away. And at some point, you will have to move out of the house. If you decide to take a little journey, don't forget those red slippers. A little click of the heels, and they will take you right to Kansas.

When will you finally give up guilt, fear, self judgment?

When you no longer see value in them. For you only think, act, and react according to what you see as valuable for you. You operate solely from self interest. Even those things which create suffering within you. Even those which appear to place a heavy veil over the face of God, over your true nature. All of these you still value in some way, giving them the power of your thought and the appearance of reality.

Why is guilt especially difficult to release?

Guilt is like the security blanket a child wakes up with every morning. It is very familiar. Because it has been with us the longest, since the appearance of the separation, it feels the most real. It hides itself well, and it is a known. Existence without guilt seems like an unknown, like you are jumping off the security of a rock. But in reality, you are chained to that rock, and it prevents you from flying. Your belief and fear around your guilt related to the separation prevent you from visiting that place inside of you which you would like to believe has been buried forever. Yet, you know that it can never be buried, and your attempt to flee from this place is what creates suffering. But this place, when seen in the Light of Truth, takes on a different meaning. You are like a person who loves to travel but who is afraid to visit an exotic world destination. When you finally go there, you see that the essence of the land and the people are the same as where you live and that you had nothing to fear. As you get close to the foundation of your deepest guilt, you can rejoice in a new destination, one where you can visit and connect with all of your peoples.

What is suffering?

Suffering is resistance to what IS. It arises from seeing and *believing* in differences which do not exist. Jesus had the experience of pain, not suffering. Although suffering is normally associated with "negative" emotions or circumstances, if you resist, you can suffer even when you experience pleasurable emotions. When you hold on to a rock or the shore, the current in the River of Life smashes into you, as opposed to it carrying you effortlessly. The stronger the current becomes, and it has now become very strong for all those who live on Earth, the greater the suffering when we resist. Eventually we become so exhausted that we let go and surrender to the River, choosing what appears to many of us as probable death through drowning. When death becomes preferable to the intense suffering created through holding on, the suffering ends. But like death, suffering is an illusion. Suffering only exists when we resist. We resist because the suffering is "painful" and we want to get out of it. One does not exist without the other, and we have the dog chasing his tail scenario. Suffering and resistance are two legs on the table of illusion. If either is taken away, the table falls. It falls out of existence completely. And the death by drowning? We do drown, but we drown in Love.

Can we avoid suffering?

We cannot avoid the appearance of suffering. The suffering, the "negative," provides the contrast to the peace and joy, the "positive." When we live as the paradox, the suffering is Itself, and the suffering is Love.

Why is forgiveness important?

Forgiveness is an illusion, because sin or error does not exist. Why is there a need to forgive something which does not exist? Yet, when you are temporarily unable to see with eyes of wholeness, and you feel like you have been "attacked" or "wronged" by another person, or you see only guilt within yourself, forgiveness is the one step within the illusion that can be taken to help restore your vision. Forgiveness shows you that the "sins" you saw in yourself or another person never existed. As with everything else on this journey, forgiveness is done purely out of self interest. For what is done by you, is done to you. When you refuse to forgive another person, you are the jailer who is keeping yourself in a prison. When you see the One, you know that forgiveness of another person is forgiveness of yourself, one of the greatest gifts that you can give to yourself. Forgiveness and gratitude give the world a glow, a gentleness that resonates with everything.

What are desires?

Desire originates from fear and the belief in separation, the need to be something different than we are. We desire different emotions, a different physical body, different life circumstances, even a different view of ourselves. When we hold these desires, we never see the perfection that we are. Yet, the desire to be different, to be something we cannot be, provides the contrast needed to illuminate the perfection that we are, so desire is another tool of Love. As the journey progresses, all desires begin to fade away, even the strong desire which propelled you on the search to know God and return to Love. You are left with only a memory of the desire, and eventually even the memory dissipates, leaving no thing.

Does choice exist?

The contrast that is needed to sustain existence is achieved through the paradox of choice. It appears that we can make choices and that there are some choices better than others. Yet, choice is impossible. There can be nothing outside of the Will of God, thus choice does not exist, or to put it another way, all choices lead to God, because all choices *are* God. We have never left our Source. God is unchanged, and our "fall" and "return" are complete. Because there was never a journey, the outcome, salvation, is certain. Once God thought it, once it was created, it was complete in the one holy moment. We have only the appearance of choice as to how we want to experience or what perception we want to operate through to reach the certain outcome, and every appearance of choice reveals Love. If a terrorist renounces violence, Love is expressed in one way. If the terrorist continues violence, Love is revealed in another way, through contrast. The appearance of what is not real is a stark contrast to what *is* Real, to Love. The appearance of choice is the manna of Life, allowing Love to recognize Itself.

So what do you do with the appearance of choices?

It is your choice how far you want to go in remembrance while you have this experience of being in a body, because every choice takes us one way or the other. If you want to go far in your remembrance, this is the place to do it. For you can only practice riding a bike if you have a bike. This earthly illusion is the bike riding arena where we practice how to be Love. It appears that the ground is full of huge boulders and all types of obstacles that make bike riding impossible, as opposed to heaven where the path is perfectly smooth. But then we realize that, just by our choice, our bike could always fly.

How do we surrender to God?

When life continually presents to you the same situation or set of circumstances, you are being offered an opportunity to have a different reaction, to see the situation a different way and to see the falsity of the belief that has produced the same reaction in you. When you do, that is surrender to God, to Love. Surrender is the passing of the belief that you have control, control over your life circumstances, control over your relationships, control over everything that you perceive as outside of you. As you deepen into the spiral, fear of God may arise, and your need for control stems directly from this fear. But then why were you created? If you have faith that you were created, then the only purpose must be so that He could Love you. True faith and surrender means that you place your future in the hands of God, knowing that whatever arises is God's Will for you. Even if it *appears* that God has abandoned you, as it appeared for Job, true faith knows that this can never be the case, that God has the grandest vision of Love for you, far beyond the comprehension of the human mind. If you believe that life and its circumstances should appear a certain way, then you have not fully surrendered. God cannot take you to the mountaintop if you are tethered down by the strings that you are trying to use to control the puppet of life. What do you have in the end? Is anything within your power? You have the power to Love. That can never be "taken away" from you. You do not have control over whether those close to you give you Love. You do not even have control of whether God loves you. But your power to express Love, no matter the circumstance or the situation, is Real. It is changeless.

Was Jesus a savior to the world?

Through his recognition and remembrance, Jesus became the Christ, he became Love. He forged the trail, leaving markers so that we would be able to follow in his footsteps, and he acts as the guide for those who choose the path of Love. Through the extreme contrast to Truth that he created by allowing himself to be put to an illusory death, he took care of our sins by showing that sin never existed. Anyone who follows the path of Love and Truth and who breaks through their limiting beliefs to see that they are not separate becomes a savior to the world, for we are One. A remembrance of that Oneness by one expression of God is shared by the whole. As Jesus was given eternal life, so was each of us. It is simply our recognition of this. Jesus took a coat of armor off the world, clearing the way so that those who followed him would only need to remove a light jacket. As he filled his role, the world waits for you to fill your role, for the puzzle cannot be completed without the piece that is you. No piece of the puzzle is more important than another. When you go into place, you become a savior for those pieces who will fit around you and you become a savior for the whole. Salvation cannot occur without *you*.

How can we use our time?

Only the present moment exists, but the illusion of time gives the appearance that each moment is brand new. And we can use that moment to Love. We can make the choice each moment of what we really want and what we want to be. The illusions of time, distance, and death take away opportunities to express Love to those mirrors close to you, your friends and family. So now is the time to express that Love, for that opportunity may not exist in the next moment. See the possibilities inherent in each moment.

What does it mean to exist in different realities simultaneously?

A single point of Light does not exist. A ray of the sun extends from its source and is not separate from all other rays extending from the sun, because they all return to the source. Each ray extends ad infinitum, and through reflection intersects with other rays. In the beginning, God created His one Son, the Christ, so that he could express His perfect Love. This ray of thought shone forth from the Mind of God, creating an infinite reflection of Love between the Father and His Son, between the Mother and Her Son, like two mirrors which are facing each other. With each reflection, the one original ray appeared to be split into smaller rays, but these sub rays were and continue to be part of the original ray, and they still extend from their Source. Each reflection creates a different reality, a different "consciousness" that is expressed through each of us. Each time we interact with another ray, each time we make a choice, we alter how the Light is reflected in the mirror, and we create another reality. Memories of "past" reflections or choices as well as an infinite number of possible "future" choices all exist simultaneously within the Mind of God. As all of the rays of God intersect, they join with each other to create a web or sea of Light. There is no place where God is not present. Each time we see this sea, we are seeing the reflection of the Source (the Father), the reflection of the Son (the Christ), the reflection of other rays (our brothers), and the reflection of our own ray. And simultaneously, all of these are seen as One. When it appears in this reality that you walk as the Son and that God is everywhere, in everyone, that it is only you and Him and that the only purpose of this reality is for Him to show you the extent of His Love, this is the way it is. When you walk in this reality and you see yourself as a manifestation of the One helping your brothers to see their ray of Light, this is the way it is. When you see only yourself in everyone and everything, this is the way it is. And when you see no rays, no differences, but only the One, this is the way it is. Jesus returned in his recognition to the original ray of Love, the Son, the Christ, which shone forth from the Mind of God. Each of us can do the same, if we so choose, at this evolutionary time of remembrance. As rays generating from the same Source, we cannot have a Will separate from that Source. Can a ray of sunshine not illuminate? Can it not warm? Can a ray of the Father not Love? The Father is the Cause. The Son is the Effect. Love begets Love.

What can we do to remember our Oneness more quickly?

You are doing something each moment you take a breath. And, of yourself you are nothing. You are perfection, yet it appears to you that you do not yet realize that perfection. Isn't all duality a state in which, by definition, we are not at full remembrance and we are working toward that remembrance? But isn't that duality still the Oneness, still the state of perfection in which the idea of change is meaningless? Can perfection be recognized without "non-perfection?" Does the paradox allow for an "answer?"

What is the only thing you cannot create?

Yourself. For you are truly a co-creator, but a split mind believes that it was borne of itself, and this belief is at the core of your thought system, creating a very unstable way of living in this experience. The result? Fear. Fear arising from the complete absence of safety. Fear of God, that this entity that is "outside" of you will destroy you. And guilt, guilt over the separation from God that arose from your illusory self creation. But how can something create itself? When you see the impossibility of this, you see that the separation never occurred and that a split mind was never created. Your Mind is restored, and you "return" to the state of Oneness from which you never separated. The result? Infinite peace. What does it mean to live this experience fully knowing yourself to be a creation of God? It means that you can finally be your Self, living as a creation of Love, without pretense, without fear, without judgment, without guilt. It means you know that you have a place in the world, a place in this unfathomable grand scheme of existence, a place as part of Creation. It means that you rest in complete safety and Stillness in the center of your being, the heart of God.

Should we be of service?

We *are* of service to the whole just by being here in this play we call Life. The Sun is incomplete without each ray. Each of us, as a unique expression of the One, is led each moment as to how we can best serve the whole, whether that be spending our life meditating in a cave, giving a smile to a stranger, serving as President of the United States, or helping the homeless. Service without regard to self, without the need to be acknowledged in any fashion in order to boost a false identity, has a great impact on bringing about a remembrance of Love, even if that act of service would appear to the world to be very minor. When we fully recognize our Oneness and we recognize that God provides for all of our needs, then our service truly becomes selfless, because then we are simply the vessel through which God acts. We can give of ourselves continually since our supply is endless. And we are giving that supply back to ourselves.

What is Truth?

Truth is universal, because only God exists, and God and Truth are the same. Yet, there are no words which can adequately describe Truth, just as God is beyond description. If you are truly living Truth and not just letting it swirl around in your head like some toy you play with, then you are experiencing its application in your whole being in each moment, in each breath you take. Truth cannot be possessed, just as God cannot be possessed.

Where can you find God?

In your heart. She has been there for an eternity, awaiting your return. When you remember this Love, you become joy and peace, and they emanate from you to everything you encounter. The proof of God's Love is everywhere around you. It is in everything you encounter, all of your experiences. It is in this book, which was given by God to you, solely to *you*. And It is in your very Existence. For why else would God have created you?

Printed in the United States
202064BV00002B/1-192/P